Mindapps

Multistate Theory
and Tools for
Mind Design

Thomas B. Roberts, Ph.D.

Park Street Press
Rochester, Vermont

Park Street Press
One Park Street
Rochester, Vermont 05767
www.ParkStPress.com

Park Street Press is a division of Inner Traditions International

Cataloging-in-Publication Data for this title is available from the Library of Congress

ISBN 978-1-62055-818-8 (print)
ISBN 978-1-62055-819-5 (ebook)

Printed and bound in the United States by McNaughton & Gunn, Inc.

10 9 8 7 6 5 4 3 2 1

Text design by Debbie Glogover and layout by Virginia Scott Bowman
This book was typeset in Garamond Premier Pro with Trenda Sans used as the display typeface

To send correspondence to the author of this book, mail a first-class letter to the author c/o Inner Traditions • Bear & Company, One Park Street, Rochester, VT 05767, and we will forward the communication, or contact the author directly on the book's Facebook page or at **troberts38@comcast.net.**

To Susan—

With love and enormous gratitude for your care.
May 30, 1982, was the luckiest day of my life, and
you've enriched every day since.

To Becca—

I'm proud of you and love you. You make me happy
to be your dad, and I look forward to seeing how you
develop your life.

To my coworkers in the psychedelic vineyards—
public and private, known and unknown, full time
and part time—who have served in this generations-
long project for public benefit from psychedelics.

Editor's Note

The reader will encounter **bolded names** and **phrases** throughout the book. Each name or phrase given in bold is linked to a numbered endnote found in the notes section, grouped by chapter. These endnotes provide information on additional resources as well as the usual source citations.

Contents

This book is about mental vastness.

Foreword

By James Fadiman, Ph.D.

Mindapps is the first book to truly address the issues we all will confront as the current "what is consciousness?" paradigm continues to dissolve and waves of new research and reported experiences accumulate.

Roberts artfully lays out the critical agenda to connect a new paradigm to a dozen fields (keep in mind that it was LSD's resemblance to serotonin that led to the explosive growth of neuroscience). The book is chock full of suggestions on how to integrate psychedelic insights and observations into a more inclusive worldview, not only of consciousness but of human inner experience, multifaceted awareness of state specific learning, and a redefinition of "identity." Roberts also describes the major issues that will need to be integrated to form a reimaging of philosophy, ethics, religions (and religious experience), and ecology, including our relationships with the natural world and the nature of death—what dies and what persists? There's even a chapter of how mind maps, derived from psychedelic experiences, could transform literary criticism.

In Roberts's vision, psychonauts will need special training, just as botanists or microbiologists or anthropologists do. He outlines the need for new forms of education to accelerate the evolution of observational science and goes on to develop how such retraining could be successfully institutionalized.

Thank you, Tom Roberts, not only for drawing the new map but also for describing how to use the tools we need for more detailed and accurate map making.

JAMES FADIMAN, PH.D., is the author of *The Psychedelic Explorer's Guide: Safe, Therapeutic, and Sacred Journeys* as well as coauthor with Jordan Gruber of the book *Healthy Selves: Who You Are and Why You Don't Know It*. Along with being an international presenter and consultant, Fadiman teaches at the Institute of Transpersonal Psychology, which he helped found in 1975. He is also the former president of the Institute of Noetic Sciences.

1
A Scent of Portent
My Journey into Mind Design

But the man who comes back through the Door in the Wall will never be quite the same as the man who went out. He will be **wiser but less cocksure,**[1]* *happier but less self-satisfied, humbler in acknowledging his ignorance yet better equipped to understand the relationship of words to things, of systematic reasoning to the unfathomable Mystery which it tries, forever vainly, to comprehend.*

ALDOUS HUXLEY,
THE DOORS OF PERCEPTION

As you read this chapter, a psychedelic intellectual autobiography, I hope you'll catch my sense of enthusiasm for ideas that psychedelics ignite. You'll notice some images of acorns and oak leaves. Why? Mighty oaks from little acorns grow. For me, the idea-acorns in this book grew into a rich interdisciplinary journey. I hope they will for you too. How did I begin?

---

*Boldfaced words and phrases lead to items listed in the notes. I enjoy skimming the list to discover what catches my eye. I hope you will enjoy it too.

LAKE TAHOE—MY FIRST TRIP, FEBRUARY 1970

Sitting on a beach in a bedraggled wicker chair, apparently left over from the previous summer and not worth taking inside for the winter. The clouds over Lake Tahoe roiled northward. Fascinating. I had never seen clouds move like that. The view along the lakefront was black and white with browns and grays, a few neon bright spots dotted the shore across the gray lake.

What was that internal sense, that powerful hidden idea that I could feel but couldn't name? "This is interesting, important, deeply meaningful, profoundly significant, enormously curious." I had never had such an experience. "What is this? What's going on here?" More than clouds and lakeshore, I strongly felt it but didn't have a word for it. Now I'd call it an intuitive sense, a kind of intellectual scent, a portent of ideas—a foreshadowing that something meaningful has happened, is happening, will happen.

For others, psychedelic portent expresses itself in works of art, music, self-revelation, helping others achieve their insights, scientific curiosity, religious enthusiasm, intellectual exploration, or sensory delight. Ideas turned out to be my path. I should have expected as much; being someone who gets captivated by ideas. My sense of portent led me toward psychedelic ideas. Focusing on psychedelics followed my habitual idea-fascinations: **behaviorism**[2] as an undergraduate at Hamilton College, the radical approach to education and child rearing espoused by A. S. Neill in his book, ***Summerhill;***[3] immediately after college and through my masters program at the University of Connecticut; and **Maslow's needs hierarchy**[4] (a model of human needs that goes from the basic and physiological to the level of transcendence) as the topic of **my doctoral dissertation**[5] at Stanford. Looking back from half a century now, I recognize that it was the scent of ideas that captivated my mind, thanks in part to a course at Stanford in the spring of 1968.

THE HUMAN POTENTIAL CLASS
AND OTHER STANFORD OPPORTUNITIES

Lake Tahoe was my first experience with psychedelics, but it wasn't my first exposure to psychedelic ideas. While I was writing my dissertation on Maslow's hierarchy of needs, I heard that professor **Willis Harman**[6]—in an oddly named department, Engineering Economic Systems—was working with Maslow's needs at Stanford Research Institute (since split off to the now independent SRI). I tried to sign up for his course Graduate Special: The Human Potential, but the seminar was so popular that I had to wait two quarters, until the spring of 1968, to be admitted. About twenty-five or so students met weekly to discuss emerging topics, many of which were fringy at the time— meditation, Eastern religions, parapsychology, yoga and the martial arts, altered states of consciousness, and so forth. At one class meeting, a married couple who were students in the class described their first LSD session the previous weekend: flowers moving in a vase, shifts in time, and difficulty in expressing their experiences. Half, maybe three-fourths of the class joined the discussion. They understood what the couple were saying. They shared their own psychedelic experiences and insights. These were advanced graduate students from Stanford's diverse graduate programs, several kinds of engineering, the arts and sciences, the humanities, professional schools, and so forth. My view was jolted. I had thought drug users were supposed to be dirty, scruffy, septic, crazy-eyed, brain-damaged misfits with inferior minds, not grad students in a select seminar at a selective university.

What was going on?! In spite of the noisy **San Francisco acid scene**,[7] the anti-psychedelic **media hype**,[8] and the government anti-drug crusade, these realistic **novelty-seeking**[9] young intellectuals were enjoying psychedelics and even implied that they benefited from them somehow. During the discussion of psychedelics, I felt like a junior member of the class. Looking back at it now, I wonder whether the

Human Potential seminar might have been the most intellectually diverse class at Stanford at that time. Perhaps ever?

Although I had signed up for Willis Harman's course to find out what he knew about Maslow's hierarchy of needs, I instead found out about psychedelics and the human potential movement. One of my fellow students was a newspaper reporter from a newspaper in Minneapolis–St. Paul who had a journalism award of some sort to attend Stanford. He had a ticket to a lecture that he couldn't use and gave it to me. At that time the **Esalen Institute**[10] in Big Sur created Esalen at Stanford. Because it cost so much for students to attend seminars in their institute along the coast, Esalen brought its presenters and group leaders to Palo Alto for weekend sessions, both scholarly and experiential. My ticket was for a lecturer whom I'd never heard of, but the ticket was free, so I decided to go. The topic was religions East and West, with comments on psychedelics. If he was boring, I thought, I could always walk out.

Erudite, charming, entertaining, witty—**Alan Watts**[11] was far from boring! My view jolted again: it was possible to think about psychedelics learnedly, philosophically, psychologically, and religiously.

Seed ideas that had been planted in my mind in Willis Harman's class and Watts's talk were germinating on the shore of Lake Tahoe, but I missed, or at least delayed, responding to other clues. Abraham Maslow was at the Laughlin Foundation in Menlo Park, almost next door to Stanford, so I asked him to serve as an outside member of my dissertation committee. He declined, saying that he would probably "crap out," meaning die. He was right. I finished my dissertation in 1972; he died in 1970. However, when I had visited his office, he told me that he was working on something new and described it a bit. I didn't catch on, but it turned out to be the needs-hierarchy level beyond **self-actualization:**[12] self-transcendence. **Maslow was interested in LSD**[13] and the **work of Stanislav Grof**.[14] Although I didn't realize it at the time because I was still working on the five-level needs-hierarchy he had created in 1954, Maslow's hints about self-transcendence, psychedelics, and transpersonal psychology lay dormant in me, to emerge intellectually after I finished my dissertation in 1972.

RAINBOWS IN VOLCANOLAND—ICELAND

Although I didn't anticipate it at Tahoe, the scent of portent led me to ideas, and by lucky chance I was invited to a meeting of major international scholars and psychotherapists discussing psychedelics at the "International Invitational Conference on Transpersonal Psychology and Psychobiology," sponsored by Geir Vilhjálmsson, head of the Institute for Consciousness Research in Reykjavík. We met in May–June 1972 at a school in **Bïfrost**,[15] a rural site in northwestern Iceland. With travel so difficult and dangerous during the winter, public schools were residential during the school year and turned into guest hotels during summer vacations.

The isolated conference site was geologically primitive, fresh, and surrounded by stark northern natural beauty. A moderate-size volcano cone rose behind the school. A massive lava escarpment ran off into the distance. The stones were volcanic cinders and boulders. Plants scratched out their existence here and there, especially in the protection of streambeds. In Icelandic, and apparently in Old Norse, Bïfrost meant "rainbow bridge to the sky," an apt metaphor for a psychedelic conference; appropriately enough, we often saw rainbows following quick short showers.

The fifty-eight invited participants came from more fields than the conference's title indicated: psychiatry, theology, comparative religions, orientology, mythology, psychosynthesis, physiology, physics, chemistry, music therapy, choreography, and dance. Most came from the United States and Canada, with nine from Iceland and a considerable contingent from Europe, including participants from England, Germany, Czechoslovakia, Italy, and France.

Starting out, I had no idea who these people were, but that soon changed. Flying there together, living together, eating together, meeting together, with none of the distractions that city-based conferences offer, and especially due to our shared interests, a sense of cohesiveness developed rapidly. Thanks to our host, Geir, we even swam together. He took us to a sort of Icelandic version of a village swimming hole; we took an hour off to swim in a lava tube filled with geothermically heated water. (However, raw lava is sharp; I still have a scar on my right foot.)

The participants composed a veritable "Who's Who" of the field.

- **Walter H. Clark.**[16] Former dean of Hartford Seminary and professor at Andover-Newton Theological Seminary, author of ***The Psychology of Religion,***[17] past president of the Society for the Scientific Study of Religion. In 1962, then a psychology professor at Andover Newton Seminary, Clark had enlisted several graduate students there to participate in the Marsh Chapel Experiment— now more informally called "**the Good Friday Experiment**"[18]— along with himself as one of the faculty/participants. His 1969 book, ***Chemical Ecstasy: Psychedelic Drugs and Religion,***[19] was the first book by a Western theologian to seriously discuss the use of psychedelics as what eventually became called *entheogens*. (*Entheogens* are "psychedelics that are intentionally used spiritually; that is, they generate (*engen*) the experience of god (*theo*) within.")

- **Joseph Campbell.**[20] When I later told a friend that I particularly enjoyed Joseph Campbell's lecture, she asked, "*The* Joseph Campbell?" I didn't know he was *the* anybody. But he was in fact the well-known world authority on myths, legends, and folktales; his book ***The Hero with a Thousand Faces***[21] was de rigueur in many college classes. Rich with slides, his lecture went up the Tibetan Buddhist chakras and down the Hindu chakras. He gave his listeners the energizing feeling that there was nothing he'd rather be doing than talking to them right there and right then.

That was my lesson on how good a good lecture can be. One that has never been surpassed.

- **Huston Smith.**[22] Author of ***The Religions of Man,***[23] "the most used book in comparative religion classes," according to a fellow conferencee, who continued, "He can get in to see the pope, the Dalai Lama, any time he wants." He went on to mention other religious leaders whose names didn't mean anything to me. In his role as one of the faculty overseers of the Good Friday Experiment, **Smith had pursued and retrieved the participant**[24] who took Rev. Howard Thurman's sermons to "go tell the world" literally and ran out of the building along Commonwealth Avenue, saw the sign "Dean of the College of Liberal Arts," and ran into the building, apparently to solicit the dean's aid in spreading the word. More recently, Smith's 2000 book, ***Cleansing the Doors of Perception: The Religious Significance of Entheogenic Plants and Chemicals,***[25] is widely recognized as a key book on entheogens by a world-respected religious scholar.

- **Stanislav Grof.**[26] The conference was organized in Iceland because it was a natural mid-ocean meeting place for North Americans and Europeans, among other reasons. The name Stanislav Grof suggested to me that he must be one of the Europeans. Originally, he was from Czechoslovakia, but in 1972, he was Director of Psychiatric Research at the Maryland Psychiatric Research Center. I had never before heard anyone describe clinical cases of LSD research and found LSD's psychotherapeutic potentials amazing. His map of the human mind was fascinating for its descriptions of what our minds are and how they operate emotionally, for what we can experience and know, and for the many ways his observations enriched the humanities, religion, psychology, and broadly conceived society and culture. His 1975 book, *Realms of the Human Unconscious: Observations from LSD Research,* compiled these ideas, mapped his view of the human mind, and is a key work in psychedelic studies.

Hearing these "greats" convinced me that it really was possible to pursue psychedelic ideas in an intellectually responsible manner. That summer I added transpersonal psychology to my graduate course in educational psychology.

While my memories of the Bïfrost conference are primarily about the ideas I encountered there, most of the participants were early psychedelic psychotherapists. They exchanged tentative professional views, techniques, insights, and recommendations. They also led us in experiential sessions. One session particularly stands out in my mind. We were lying down on the floor of the large meeting space while one of the psychotherapists led us in an exercise in progressive relaxation, imagery, and self-suggestion. Then she played the *St. Cecilia Mass* by Charles Gounod. It was magnificent. Still enfolded in a light trance, I got up and looked through a large picture window. The raw volcanic landscape was bursting alive in the arctic spring. It gave me a sense of what the nature poets meant by *sublime*. Although I didn't realize it at the time, experiencing an altered state of consciousness via a method other than a psychedelic prepared me to recognize other mindbody* methods.

VOLUNTARY CONTROL OF INTERNAL STATES—COUNCIL GROVE

Many of us who had attended the Bïfrost conference in the spring of 1972 rented a ski lodge together at the "1972 Annual Meeting of the Association for Humanistic Psychology" in September at Squaw Valley, California. My curiosity was piqued when I overheard some of our group and their friends talking about "Council Grove," as in "See you at Council Grove." What was that? It sounded like an insider sort of thing, and I wanted to be included. I learned that Council Grove was the

---

*Mindbody methods are those that nurture *mindbody states:* overall patterns of cognitive and bodily functioning, composed of body plus mind considered as one unified whole, not as different things closely interacting. Thus, the hyphen in *mind-body* is dropped.

familiar name for a series of conferences whose title was Conference on the Voluntary Control of Internal States. According to rumors I heard later, participant John Lilly* asserted that "voluntary control of internal states" meant that anyone could do any drugs anytime they wanted.

Sponsored by the Menninger Foundation, the Conferences on the Voluntary Control of Internal States were held annually, beginning in 1969, at White Memorial Camp, a church camp near the village of Council Grove, Kansas. As with the Icelandic meeting, the location was isolated, in this case on an otherwise wide-open prairie. Again, this forced participants to spend concentrated time together not only during presentations but also through their dining and living arrangements in camp bunkhouses.

As an incubator of new ideas that weren't ready yet to be accepted into the mainstream scientific and medical paradigms, Council Grove provided a place to try out emerging ideas. In a safe atmosphere, presenters gained critiques and suggestions from other participants so as to refine their ideas and presentations for later publications and talks at formal professional conferences. To encourage a free-for-all of raw ideas and open-minded speculation, Council Grove proceedings weren't published; although **four general reports**[27] appeared.

At Squaw Valley, I didn't find out much about Council Grove, but I knew I wanted to attend. Attendance was limited to the number of bunks at the campground, however. How could I get invited? Luck struck again. By an odd quirk in funding, my university department received some unexpected funding during the 1972–1973 academic year. I applied for a grant to fund a conference, and it was funded. Council Grove was held every year during the week after Easter, so I planned the first "Conference on Applications of Transpersonal Psychology to Education" to meet immediately after Council Grove and invited many of the Council Grove people to present, given that they were already in

---

*John Lilly was a physician, neuroscientist, psychoanalyst, psychonaut, philosopher, writer, inventor, and researcher into the nature of consciousness, using mainly isolation tanks, dolphin communication, and psychedelic drugs, sometimes in combination.

the Midwest. It worked. The next year I was invited and attended for two additional years, until the series ended, to be replaced by a conference that specialized in "energy"—*energy* in the psychological sense, not oil, gas, or wind. Although I didn't realize it at the time, thanks to Council Grove, my view of the human mind expanded greatly.

Elmer and Alyce Green,[28] of the Menninger Foundation, co-creators of the conference, specialized in biofeedback, which at the time was widely dismissed: so-called well-informed people "knew" that it was impossible to voluntarily control the autonomic nervous system and endocrine system. Other new and exploratory ideas were welcome there too: progressive relaxation, imagery and visualization, hypnosis, meditation and Eastern religious practices, a variety of psychoactive drugs, Native American spiritual practices, therapeutic touch, massage, yoga and the martial arts, Asian medicines, acupuncture, chanting and breathing exercises, various forms of bodywork, and so forth. Anomaly-friendly participants discussed psychic phenomena, near-death experiences, and out-of-the-body reports.

Hearing these topics discussed with both scientific skepticism and open-minded speculation broadened my view of ways to explore consciousness beyond psychedelics, and eventually led me to see psychedelics as one collection of methods among many, but still my favorite one.

THE MIDNIGHT SUN—INARI, FINLAND

The midseventies were a fertile time for nurturing additional ideas. Following the 1972 Bïfrost meeting, in 1975 Geir organized the "Second International Invitational Conference on Transpersonal Psychology and Society." In my CV, I have the location as Lojosaratnsskart, Iceland, but I haven't been able to find the town on a map of Iceland or on Google, even with adjustments in spelling. Many people from the first meeting attended, and the places of others were filled by some Council Grove people, others from the Association for Transpersonal Psychology, and more from Europe. Again, our cohesion increased thanks to living together in an isolated school.

There was talk of a third meeting in another three years, but one bunch of us didn't want to wait so long, so we decided to form another group and have one in 1976. Most of our group were from Scandinavia (broadly considered geographically and genealogically), so we jokingly called ourselves "the Scandinavian renegades." At some time during the planning, I mentioned that one of my school textbooks had a series of photographs that showed the midnight sun at stages all the way around a horizon, and I hoped that our conference the next year could take place at a midnight sun time and location.

The main organizers were Leo Matos, a Brazilian living in Denmark, and Beni Furman, a Finnish medical school student, and his many friends. The Finns arranged for us to celebrate twenty-four hours of sunlight at the "Midnight Sun International Conference on Transpersonal Psychology." We met in another off-session school on June 24–29, 1976, near Lake Inari in the far north conifer woods of Finland, and I got to see the midnight sun over several days. As in Iceland and Council Grove, Inari's rural woodsy setting promoted group cohesiveness. The largest contingent by far were Finns, with fewer Americans, and more Europeans, thanks to easier travel. Prince Peter of Denmark brought a group of Tibetan monks who had sought refuge in Denmark, and they stretched the scope of our ideas by participating in several sessions.

The Inari meeting went so well, we wanted to continue in future years. There already was a Transpersonal Institute and an Association for Transpersonal Psychology (ATP) with its *Journal of Transpersonal Psychology,* made up largely of Americans; in fact, *JTP*'s first issue listed the "American Transpersonal Association." To geographically broaden its scope, we organized the **International Transpersonal Association,**[29] and—to encourage people with broader disciplinary interests to feel welcome—we dropped "psychology" from its name. Stan Grof agreed to be our first president. Two years later ITA jelled into a formal organization.

SPROUTING IDEAS IN THE 1980s

Stanford, Tahoe, Iceland, Council Grove, Finland—together they seeded a hybrid line of ideas: humanistic psychology → transpersonal psychology → consciousness → drug policy → psychedelics → entheogens → multistate mind. In the 1980s, the seeds sprouted.*

1981—The First Psychedelics Course in Higher Education

In 1981, I started teaching my psychedelics course. Its original title was Psychedelic Research, but some students thought "research" implied that the course would have too many statistics so they didn't take it. So I changed its name to Psychedelic Mindview. I think it underwent several other name changes from time to time. I hoped and expected that once I taught a psychedelics course at Northern Illinois University that other professors would start similar courses at their colleges and universities. I broke the ice, but there weren't any other boats.

Each semester I taught the course as a one-off, temporary special topic course until the early 2000s. Then, my assistant department chair said that it was time to make it a regular catalog course; temporary courses were supposed to be limited to only three years, not twenty. So I went through the usual curriculum process, which included only one impeding bump. To reflect the name of our department, the title became Foundations of Psychedelic Studies in Education. "Foundations" was part of our departmental name, and "in Education" was because it was in the College of Education; that kept the College of Liberal Arts and Science off our backs for infringing on their territory, not that I saw any likelihood that they had any interest in psychedelics. Briefly, it had the course number 420. Neither my assistant chair nor I real-

---

*Wherever the symbol "→" appears in this book, it stands variously for "produces," "results in," "yields," "leads to," and "equals."

ized that the number **420**[30] had strong marijuana associations, but in our department, 420 was already being used for a different course, so it ended up with 426. Too bad!

1981—Litcrit and Psychocriticism

With my own background of having been an undergraduate English major, I naturally connected my psychological and psychedelic explorations to literature. So I submitted an article to *The CEA Critic,* an official journal of the College English Association, **"Consciousness Criticism,"**[31] which appeared in the thematic edition *The Academy and the Mind: I.* In it I proposed three varieties of psychocriticism: consciousness, transpersonal, and Grofian (referring to the approach of Stanislav Grof, one of the world's foremost psychedelic researchers).

1982—The Loonie

During the summer of 1982, I taught at the Ontario Institute for Studies in Education, a home of bright students and friendly colleagues in a lively city. Sometime later when a new $1 Canadian coin appeared, it had a loon on the back and a likeness of Her Majesty on the front. After I returned to Northern Illinois University in DeKalb, Illinois, I wrote a letter-to-the-editor of the *Toronto Star* suggesting that the coin be nicknamed "the loony two" for its two loons, back and front. I never saw the letter in print, but apparently my letter was printed, as I soon received a letter from a royalist who thought that I should have shown more respect to Her Majesty. If Her Majesty reads this, I much belatedly do apologize. Although I intended "the loony two" just for the $1 coin, apparently the name caught on as the current $2 Canadian currency is called "the toonie." I apologize to all Canadians who touch their specie.

1983—Coming Out of the Psychedelic Closet

It was with some trepidation that I faced the publication of the book *Psychedelic Reflections,*[32] to which I had been invited to contribute a chapter. In it I mentioned for the first time that I had actually done psychedelics. This step out of the psychedelic closet came about from an invitation from Jake Bakalar, whom I had met in the spring of 1978 as a fellow seminarian in a monthlong seminar titled "Frontiers of Science" (nicely vague), led by Stan and Christina Grof at Esalen Institute. James "Jake" Bakalar was coauthor with Lester Grinspoon of *Psychedelic Drugs Reconsidered,* a book that I still consult. I worried. What would my colleagues think? What about people "across campus"? How might the public react? Should I respond to their reactions? I didn't want to be seen as the Timothy Leary of Northern Illinois University.

The book came out . . . no reaction. I listed it on my annual evaluation form . . . no reaction. No big deal! Considering that I was already teaching my psychedelics course, I suppose they had already figured it out. What was a big thing to me was insignificant to others. Like so many people then, and even now, I built up my own apprehension. Based on my experience, my advice is: be brave. In fact it doesn't take much bravery at all. You'll probably get a big yawn.

1984—Dear DEA

On the morning of April 13th, Rick Doblin of MAPS called me. He was organizing a group of professionals to petition the Drug Enforcement Administration to hold hearings on the scheduling of MDMA. They intended to schedule it along with heroin and other dangerous drugs with no medical uses into Schedule I of the Controlled Substances Act.

Although we had met and corresponded earlier, this was the first of Rick's projects that I became involved in. Starting then and growing since, I admire his unbounded energy, optimism, and lifelong, selfless dedication to human benefit.

As soon as Rick called, I got up, went into my office, and wrote the **first letter**[33] of Rick's MDMA campaign to the DEA. I wish I had kept their reply; it was standard bureaucratese, recognizing that as a citizen I had a right to request a hearing. My co-petitioners were Lester Grinspoon, a psychiatrist at Harvard Medical School and recognized scholar of psychoactive drugs; pharmacist June Riedlinger; and George Greer, a psychiatrist who did an early pilot study of the subjective effects of MDMA. I had been one of his volunteers. This caught the DEA by surprise, and, as they phrased it, a drug had recruited some defenders. Administrative law judge Frances Young presided. An administrative law judge is a government official charged with evaluating the evidence, in this case on rescheduling. He found that MDMA had established medical benefits with low to moderate potential for abuse and should be on Schedule III. After such a hearing, the DEA is then supposed to take the findings into account when they schedule. However, a new head of the DEA, John Lawn, who had been an upper-level FBI agent, but with no medical training or experience, ignored Judge Young's findings and placed MDMA in Schedule I. **An opinion piece**[34] covers this and related problems with scheduling.

1985—Bicycle Day

As with most of my ideas, I didn't sense a problem then try to find a solution. As usual, when the idea of a day to celebrate psychedelics popped in my head, it immediately felt right; I later discovered or made up reasons for it. No need to go through my rationalizations. You either see and feel it or you don't. Contrary to what I suppose many people imagine, **Bicycle Day**[35] (see appendix C) celebrations were not heavy drug-taking days but were more like family gatherings. There were always children present. Whether it took place inside or outside our house, or both, mostly depended on the weather. A particularly skilled craftsman-artist brought artifacts—one year it was a bicycle windmill on a pole, another year it was a globe with a swarm of bicycles around it. Most fun of all was when it was a cylinder of helium so we could take turns jumping our voice pitches up a couple notches. Then we filled balloons, tied messages to Albert Hofmann* on them, and let

---

*On April 19, 1943, Albert Hofmann first intentionally tried LSD; he rode home on a bicycle, a very memorable (now celebrated) ride, since he was still "under the influence."

them go. We had no pretense that they'd get to him in Switzerland, but it was fun. To my delight, Bicycle Day caught on with events here and there around the world, and articles and news stories mention Bicycle Day.

I consider my ideas—those in this book are the current prime ones—to be my major contribution to the field, but it looks more and more like Bicycle Day will outrank them. Still, it does give me an inner warm glow of satisfaction to see Bicycle Day catching on.

1986—MAPS (Multidisciplinary Association for Psychedelic Studies)

Rick Doblin was founding an organization and tried out some ideas for its name with me. Would we use *interdisciplinary, cross-disciplinary,* or something else? Obviously *multidisciplinary* won. And it gives a nice abbreviation for a forward-looking group too. My guess (and I'm not at all sure of this) is that *studies* rather than *medicine, psychology,* or *therapy* was my contribution, just as I had suggested *studies* in Finland for the International Association for Transpersonal Studies so as to encourage a wide range of people and ideas. So I became a founding member of MAPS, and every year I increase my gratitude to Rick for carrying the torch of psychedelic studies through the dark years. Now the torch has burst into a leading light in psychedelic psychotherapy. As you'll see in this book, I continue to like consciousness *studies* and mind *studies*.

1987—Grofian Psychocriticism, Snow White

This is the story of how I got interested in using the ideas of Stan Grof as a way to understand the arts, society, and much more. As is often the case at professional meetings, it's the chance meeting and informal chat that is most productive. It was that way at Council Grove too. Probably following a discussion of the seven chakras at lunch one day, our discussion moved to the number seven. One of my companions mentioned that seven often had magical connotations that appeared across cultures and that the Grimm brothers' seven dwarfs were a well-known example.

I didn't pay much attention to it, but when I returned home after the conference, Disney's *Snow White and the Seven Dwarfs* was playing at a local theater. That warmed up my thinking again about the mythic part of our minds. By coincidence my graduate class was reading Grof's *Realms of the Human Unconscious* that week. Click! I saw that his map of our minds (see fig. 5.1 on page 60) fit *Snow White*. We made a class field trip to the movie theater. The theater staff must have wondered about a group of graduate students who showed up for an evening performance of a children's movie, bought tickets, and sat together, whispering, nodding, and smiling during the movie.

Grofian psychocriticism—which will be explored in detail in chapter 5—is a rich field of ideas for many disciplines. Although in 1986, I published an article on the movie **Brainstorm**[36] and had previously lectured on my interpretation of *Snow White*—first at the 1979 Association for Transpersonal Psychology Annual Meeting, second in 1980 at the "Sixth Annual Holistic Health Conference" in San Diego, then at Council Grove in 1981—I still consider my 1987 published article on the movie **Snow White**[37] to be the real beginning of my Grofian psychocriticism.

1988—Multistate

At the "Tenth International Transpersonal Association Conference" in Santa Rosa, California, the influences of Council Grove, Finland, and other international contacts finally caught up with me. I gave a one-and-a-half-hour lecture on "Multistate Education" that marked a broader view of our minds; psychedelics became one family of what I now call *mindapps*. I proposed an education that included all of what I now call *mindbody states*. The following year *The Journal of Transpersonal Psychology* printed "**Multistate Education:** Metacognitive Implications of the Mindbody Psychotechnologies,"[38] which claimed that "there is much more to human capacity than is ordinarily imagined, even more than some people in the 'human potential movement' have accepted." This book extends those ideas.

1989—ATE SPECIAL INTEREST GROUP

Like other professional organizations, the Association of Teacher Educators (ATE) has divisions and smaller special interest groups (SIGs). Jerry L. Fletcher and I thought that ATE would benefit from a Transpersonal and Humanistic SIG, so we founded one. At that time, Jerry was Senior Policy Analyst in Education for the Department of Health, Education, and Welfare. The SIG existed for a few years then decided its interests overlapped with the Affective Education SIG, and so merged into it.

ENTER MINDAPPS

Half a century after the Human Potential class, after the scent of portent, after all the intervening events, where has this taken me? Thanks to Willis Harman and the Human Potential class at Stanford, I learned that drug takers are not scrambled-brain, drug-crazed, dope fiends—at least some of them aren't—and that an internationally renowned scholar could find them worth his attention. Thanks to my Lake Tahoe experience plus more than a hundred similar ones since, psychedelics boosted my curiosity, introducing me to interlocking parts of the neurosciences, the arts and literature, mythology, anthropology, the ancient classical period, social relations, history, enthnography, botany, philosophy, religion, health, policy, and law. Thanks to Council Grove, I realized that besides psychedelics there are also many other psychotechnologies. Thanks to the "Midnight Sun" conference, my colleagues, sources of ideas, and conferences have widened internationally.

In a vague, general sort of way, the scent of portent has taken me on a parallel course to a four-year undergraduate program with every year expanded into a decade. In the seventies, my first decade, I got my intellectual feet wet by meeting people and getting to know organizations, sort of who's who and what's where. The eighties encouraged me to try many new things—some lasted; others didn't. In my third decade, the nineties, I found my interest in drug policy and especially religious liberty focusing on entheogens. In the first decade of the twenty-first century I developed my entheogenic interests further, then realized that they connected me to a still wider multistate view, one that needed new ideas, new ways of looking at things, and a fresh vocabulary to express them.

Most strongly, taken together as a whole, the past half century of ideas and experiences has intensified my curiosity about what our minds are and what they might become, and I've coined words and phrases that are the faces of the ideas with which I'm working. It would be nice to be able to say that ideas occur to me while tripping, but that would be wishful thinking. Typically my mind manifests ideas between 2:00 and 4:00 a.m., and they don't first appear as ideas but rather as words or phrases that I immediately recognize as ones that feel right, "Yes. That's what I want to say." *Scrambled-brain,* above, is an example. Words are the faces of ideas; after recognizing that they feel right and as I use them, I realize that it's the ideas behind those face-words that I'm really after. Following these intellectual scents, what ideas have I sniffed out? *Psychedelic* means "mind-manifesting." Minds manifest ideas; so psychedelic minds manifest psychedelic ideas. What ideas did my mind manifest?

- *Ideagen.* Recognizing that psychedelics stimulate ideas, I coined the term *ideagen* to use when they do so. *Ideagen* is not a synonym for *psychedelic.* It refers to psychedelics only in their function of generating ideas.
- *Mindapp.* Psychedelics function in our brain-mind complex as

mindapps. That is, just as we can write and install digital apps in our electronic devices, we can construct mindapps and install them in our brain-mind complex. Similarly, just as apps increase the power and uses of our devices, mindapps increase the power and uses of our minds.

- *Multistate theory.* Besides psychedelics there are many other families of mindapps—many kinds of, say, meditation, hypnosis, martial arts, brain stimulations, breathing techniques, neurofeed-back and biofeedback, synthetic biology—the list goes on and on, and new ones are being invented and imported every day. Seeing these many kinds of mindapps all as part of a single, large, inclusive view of our minds produces multistate theory.

- *Mind design.* We usually use mindapps one at a time. When we combine them in new recipes, we will produce mindstates that have never before been produced—*mind design*. The human mind becomes a research variable.

- *MindappAI.* Our default, ordinary mind-brain complex produces our intelligence and all of our other mental processes. When we combine mindapps, will we produce new kinds of mindstates, new kinds of cognition, perception, and other mental and bodily abilities? Will these new states contain *mindapp-based artificial intelligence*? What ideas might occur? What rare and unknown abilities may reside there?

Where will my psychedelic-inspired intellectual exploration take you? Who can say for sure, but I do want you to know what to expect from this book. In the second chapter, we will explore in some depth a number of these ideas, contrasting what I term the *singlestate fallacy* with *multistate theory,* offering a more complete view of the human mind, contrasting the terms *mindbody state* and *state of consciousness,* as well as looking at many applications of mindapps. In chapter 3, we'll add the idea *mindappAI* (mindapp artificial intelligence). It will stretch us to peer into the unlimited future frontiers of mind design, as it proposes that mindapps, both psychedelic and non-psychedelic, can be combined to form new, artificial mindbody states in the brain-mind complex. Thus, the future of the human mind is unlimited.

In Western society during the past one hundred years, psychedelics have evolved—and are continuing to evolve—in three stages. First and predominantly, they have been adjuncts to psychotherapy. Second and to a lesser extent, they are becoming adjuncts to spiritual development. Are there additional ways to think about drug studies in general and psychedelics in particular? Do psychedelic-derived ideas open additional ways to explore, understand, and use our minds? Keeping in mind that conceptual research requires us to show how our new ideas help us think better—are "fruitful"—chapters 4 through 8 illustrate how reconceiving drug studies supports new adventures in scientific, humanistic, religious, educational, and cultural thinking.

The conclusion pulls these ideas together to demonstrate that multistate theory meets seven of the eight criteria of a **paradigm shift**[39] as derived from Thomas Kuhn's *The Structure of Scientific Revolutions*. As chapters 3 through 8 show, beyond updating of drug studies, drug laws, and **drug policies,**[40] multistate theory reformulates what it means to have a mind, enriches what our minds can do, and informs our views of the sciences, humanities, arts, and religion.

With these opportunities in mind, in the appendices, I offer three creative ways to spread the benefits of mindapps more widely. In appendix A, I encourage you to start your own psychedelics course and provide you with my last syllabus to adapt as you see fit. Appendix B, Psychedelics Without Borders: Notes for a Business Prospectus, suggests just one part of an answer to the question "What is the fastest way for the largest number of people to benefit most quickly from psychedelic-assisted psychotherapy?" And more than this, it answers the questions "How do we raise the vast sums necessary for research and eventual federal approval?" and "Can we recruit the financial community's support for psychedelic research, approval, and treatment?" Appendix C tells the story of the origins of Bicycle Day. Ride on.

This is a book for people who have a taste for ideas. Using multistate concepts as ingredients, what flavorful ideas will bake in your mind? Read on.

2
Augmenting Human Intellect with Mindapps

Introducing Multistate Theory

By "augmenting human intellect" we mean increasing the capability of a man to approach a complex problem situation, to gain comprehension to suit his particular needs, and to derive solutions to problems. . . . We refer to a way of life in an integrated domain where hunches, cut-and-try, intangibles, and the human "feel for a situation" usefully co-exist with powerful concepts, streamlined terminology and notation, sophisticated methods and high-powered electronic [read "mindapp"] aids.

DOUGLAS C. ENGELBART,
"AUGMENTING HUMAN INTELLECT:
A CONCEPTUAL FRAMEWORK"

The psychotherapeutic uses of psychedelics are widely known, their biological functions are increasingly characterized, and their entheogenic uses are becoming recognized, but as generators of ideas—

ideagens—they are largely unknown. When a common definition of science—observation + theory → science—is applied to the application of psychedelics to intellectual pursuits, it spotlights this lack. Current data is strong, but theory is underweight. Conceptual research addresses this lack; it invents concepts, refines them, then demonstrates their fruitfulness. This chapter starts that process in relation to psychedelics.

In this chapter, we'll look at ideas derived from psychoactive drug research, primarily psychedelics, but those ideas widen to take us far beyond psychedelics to a fuller view of what our minds are and what they are capable of becoming. This is expressed by what I have labeled *multistate theory*.

Basic Ideas in
the Multistate Theory

1. Because of the ambiguity of the word *consciousness,* in the multi-state theory the word *mindbody* replaces *consciousness* when it refers to overall patterns of mind plus body functioning at any one time, and *mindbody state* replaces *state of consciousness.*

2. *Mindapps* are methods of altering overall patterns of biological, behavioral, and cognitive processes. Just as we can write digital apps and install them in our electronic devices, we can create bio-information mindapps and install them in our brain-mind complex.

3. When we ask if there are other mindapps besides psychedelic ones, we recognize many other mindapp families, thus generating multistate theory.

4. *Residence* is the recognition that all behavior and experience reside in (are expressions of) their respective mindbody states.

5. What I have designated the *central multistate question* promotes new hypotheses, research agendas, questions, and methods.

6. *Mind design*—recipes for combining several mindapps—will

produce new, previously never-experienced, "artificial" mind-body states.

7. *MindappAI* will extend the human brain-mind complex and contain previously unknown human experiences and capabilities. If systematically pursued, this founds a new intellectual activity.

We'll start off by discussing the erroneous assumption that all good thinking takes place only in our default, ordinary mindbody state. From a period in which the focus was on describing, prescribing, and augmenting the human mind in its ordinary default state (awake), we are advancing to a new era of mind design. Briefly, we can increase the repertoire of our mental processes—sensory and cognitive, physiological and mental, conscious and unconscious—by installing a large and constantly increasing number of what I call *mindapps* in our brain-mind system. This advance produces new research questions and paradigms, refreshes approaches to standard scientific and humanistic topics, and broadens the wider intellectual world by opening the door to our minds' greater futures. Because psychedelics are receiving so much scientific, professional, and media attention, and because they are the most dramatic type of mindapps, this book uses them to exemplify the wider field of mindapps and to illustrate the fruitfulness of the multistate theory.

THE SINGLESTATE FALLACY

What I call the *singlestate fallacy* is the major theoretical impediment to the multistate theory. It is the hegemonic assumption that all worthwhile thinking takes place only in our ordinary, default mindbody state. It assumes that other mindbody states contain no knowledge and have no practical uses.

I have to admit to a bit of skullduggery at this point. In talking with professors, I've found many who readily admit it when I point out that their own contributions and their disciplines usually fail to consider other mindbody states ("states of consciousness" as they like to call them). But it's hard to get them to do anything about it; they just go on omitting the range our minds can span. But *making a fallacy* is a dreaded scholarly no-no. In some disciplines a fallacy is just an embarrassment. In others, a misdemeanor. To psychologists, cognitive fallacies are felonies, and to philosophers fallacies are a crime. So using the word *fallacy* is my devious tactic. I hope it can get my fellow academics to correct their omissions and pay more attention to the many mindbody states our minds can achieve and use.

The so-called singlestate fallacy meets Kuhn's observation that an existing dominant paradigm "can **insulate a community** from those socially important problems that are not reducible"[1] to their usual way of thinking. The singlestate fallacy's insulation still continues in spite of "the plethora of new studies and published papers in the scientific press" and "multiple pilot studies demonstrating their efficacy and safety," according to Dr. Ben Sessa, a psychiatrist and medical author from Bristol, England. He adds, "Other impediments include a prevailing **attitude of pseudoscience** and rigidity from within the non-scientific community itself."[2]

A Distillation of Thomas Kuhn's
Scientific Revolutions Theory

1. A new paradigm includes previously excluded phenomena.
2. A new paradigm posits new relationships among the newly included phenomena and concepts.
3. A new paradigm introduces useful concepts.
4. A new paradigm accepts and helps explain some anomalies.
5. A new paradigm stimulates new research questions and agendas (new normal science).

6. A new paradigm provides new variables, treatments, and methodologies.

7. A new paradigm strengthens professional preparation.

8. A new paradigm must include a group of professionals who intentionally use this paradigm.

Thanks to a rapidly filling reservoir of evidence though, research on meditation and psychedelic research breaks through that isolation and destroys the singlestate fallacy through a variety of avenues. As the section "A Mindapp Population Boom" on page 34 considers, mindapp discovery and research cover a vast range of traditional and emerging fields. Solving scientific and business problems, informing the arts and humanities, asking new questions, reframing current fields of knowledge, and providing new research methods qualify psychedelics as a new paradigm. Thanks to psychedelic and other mindapp-generated ideas, these diverse fields are already fruitful, although to different extents. Philosophers and others who off-handedly dismiss psychedelics and other mindapps as empirically vacant have psychedelic-generated innovative ideas and practical benefits to explain away. To unroll the full prospect of this vision, it helps to see psychedelics as part of a more inclusive view of our minds.

Psychotherapy

As the most researched area in psychedelics, psychotherapy leads the way. Psychedelic psychotherapy's benefits are increasingly reported in professional publications and in the general press. Among professional organizations, the following are my **favorites**.[3]

- Beckley Foundation
- Council on Spiritual Practices
- Erowid
- Heffter Research Institute

- Imperial College
- Multidisciplinary Association for Psychedelic Studies
- Núcleo de Estudos Interdisciplinares sobre Psicoativos

The information on psychotherapy and the neurosciences on the websites offered by these organizations and other sources meet one of the criteria for a new paradigm: "First the new candidate must seem to **resolve some outstanding and generally recognized problem[s]** that can be solved no other way."[4] Although Kuhn had scientific problems in mind, resolving problems applies as well to psychedelic-assisted psychotherapy. The organizations listed above report promising early studies of psychedelic-assisted psychotherapy and post-traumatic stress disorder, addictions, depression, and anxiety, among others.

Arts and Humanties

Psychedelic inspiration in music and the visual arts goes far beyond popular culture's psychedelic posters. Reminiscent of the early twentieth-century arts and crafts movement, psychedelic-inspired **folk craft**[5] of the 1960s featured natural products and wood finishes with inspiration from art nouveau in elaborate embroidery designs. Psychedelics have influenced **art**[6] with intensified color, incongruous objects, and distorted shape arising from artists' unconscious. **Design,**[7] **music,**[8] and films, as well as literature and philosophy have their "on acid" schools. Chapters 4 through 8 present nuggets and clues unearthed by clinical researchers for the arts and humanities to consider.

Problem-Solving

Problem-solving divides into two distinct routes, **microdosing**[9] (taking very small doses, usually 10 to 20 micrograms of LSD every few days to increase one's ordinary functioning) and **psychedelic creative problem-solving,**[10] taking moderate doses for a daylong session addressed to specific problems. Of course, both these qualify as ideagen methods too. The epitome of solving professional problems comes from

1966 when twenty-seven engineers, architects, scientists, and other professionals used daylong structured mescaline sessions to solve forty-four persistently unsolved professional problems (most fully described in James Fadiman's 2011 book, *The Psychedelic Explorer's Guide*). Solutions ranged from the aesthetic-spatial design of a chair and a building, to figuring out a theoretical physics problem, to solving an advanced wiring problem. Jumping forward half a century, Aeylet Waldmans's 2017 classic, *A Really Good Day,* reports that microdosing with LSD sharpened her ability to focus on her professional writing and enhanced her relationships with her children and husband. Can it be any wonder that leading-edge electronic inventors today are widely rumored to boost their creativity with these productive mindapps?

Religion

As psychedelic mystical experiences are informing religious texts and practices (or even replacing them), old sacraments are being reborn and new ones invented. The rich history of mindapps starts in prehistoric times and stretches through ancient Greece and St. Thomas Aquinas to today's fascination with the Amazonian tea ayahuasca. This connection between psychedelics and religion is not just a hippy holdover from the '60s: the subtitle of eminent philosopher of religion Huston Smith's *Cleansing the Doors of Perception*: *The Religious Significance of Entheogenic Plants and Chemicals* states the connection clearly. Chapter 8 of this book fills in the details and develops the entheogenic quest by speculating that we may be going through another reformation, this one based on entheogens, that may serve today's "nones" and "spiritual but not religious" people too.

Humanities

Although the liberal arts are still snoozing when it comes to psychedelics, psychedelic clinical research has uncovered rich nuggets that intersect the humanities' domains: the nature of mind, insights/ideas, meaningfulness, spirituality, mystical experiences, sense of self, ego-transcendence, archetypes, ancestral memories, creativity, sense of "other," noetic knowing, artistic performance and appreciation, aesthetics, and more. As chapter 5 shows, psychocriticism derived from Grof's early clinical research brings additional meanings to art, movies, mythology, the rhetoric of war, philosophy, religion, and literature. If psychedelics are used skillfully to occasion mystical experiences, they can **raise values and moral development**[11] and promote **open-mindedness.**[12]

The title of Ben Sessa's 2017 book captures this wider psychotherapeutic and cultural movement, ***The Psychedelic Renaissance: Reassessing the Role of Psychedelic Drugs in 21st Century Psychiatry and Society.***[13]

THE MULTISTATE THEORY— TOWARD A COMPLETE VIEW OF THE HUMAN MIND

In contrast to the singlestate fallacy, the multistate theory recognizes that the ability to produce and use a variety of mindbody states is a significant human trait, and multistate phenomena deserve their place in our studies of the human mind. This is not to denigrate our knowledge of our ordinary, default state. Far from discarding existing information, a new paradigm "must **promise to preserve** a relatively large part of the concrete problem-solving ability that has accrued to science through its predecessors."[14] Multistate theory encompasses our ordinary state and especially values it as the mindbody state that has been most thoroughly studied. Our existing singlestate findings contribute to a whole multistate map of our minds, and established research on our usual, default state sets high standards for methods, questions, and topics that the nascent studies of other states might emulate.

The shift to the multistate theory produces three basic concepts:

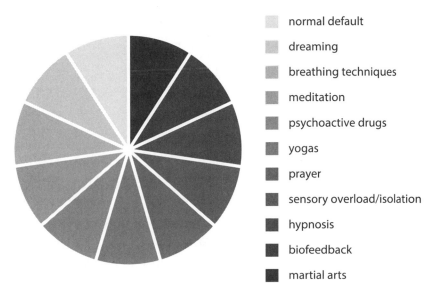

normal default

dreaming

breathing techniques

meditation

psychoactive drugs

yogas

prayer

sensory overload/isolation

hypnosis

biofeedback

martial arts

Fig. 2.1. Multistate theory. A complete view of our minds must include all the mindbody states created by mindapps.

- mindbody state
- mindapps and metaintelligence
- residence and the central multistate question

Basically, these ideas are fun to think with.

Mindbody State and the Clarification of Consciousness

As mentioned earlier, *mindbody states* are overall patterns of cognitive and bodily functioning at any one time. They are composed of body plus mind considered as one unified whole, not as different things closely interacting. Thus, the hyphen in *mind-body* is dropped. Dropping the hyphen is a small typographical change, but in the multistate theory, *mindbody* without the hyphen emphasizes that we're considering over-all, unified patterns taken as a whole. I'm not saying that *mind-body* is any kind of mistake; it's just the word when you want to denote two separate things that are closely related.

The most common default state is wakefulness, with sleeping and dreaming also common. Most of the time we habitually use our default state to think with; this applies when we think about everything in the universe and even when we think about that state itself. Under a multi-state theory, studies of all other mindbody states move from the periphery of discourse to its center: current mind-related questions become re-asked *for* all other states and *in* all other states.

The word *mindbody* also avoids the ambiguity of the word *consciousness,* which is used in different ways in different disciplines and in common language. Confusion arises when different people who use the word *consciousness* think that they are all talking about the same thing. Even worse, among many writers, *consciousness* often seems to be a meaningless placeholder of a word that is chosen because it sounds profound but when unpacked is hollow. Anyone using *consciousness* needs to specify their meaning. The following list of the primary uses of the word *consciousness* makes it clear that the meanings are quite different, though at times overlapping.

- Common language 1—*Conscious[ness]* means awake and interacting normally with the environment. For example, "She is *conscious* now, but last night she was asleep," and "After being in a coma for three days, he is *conscious.*"
- Common language 2—*Consciousness* refers to what one habitually thinks about, to what is typically "on one's mind," such as "She has strong ecological *consciousness,*" or "Money occupies the center of his *consciousness.*"
- Politics and the social sciences—*Consciousness* means the thoughts and feelings one has constructed due to one's place in society, such as *proletarian consciousness* or *women's consciousness.*
- Philosophy—*Consciousness* refers to a self-reflective sense of "I": one thinks and can reflect on oneself and on one's thinking. In this case, the word *self-reflexiveness* would be more precise and avoid ambiguity.

- Religion and spiritual discussions—*Consciousness* means level of spiritual development, as in "His mystical experience raised John's level of consciousness."
- Psychology 1—*Consciousness* is the sequence of what one attends to second by second; what passes through one's mind becomes the *stream of consciousness.*
- Psychology 2—Here *consciousness* refers to different overall patterns of mind and body functioning at any one time, as in **"altered states of consciousness."**[15]

My point is not that *consciousness* is an undesirable word, but that when people use it, they should be clear about what they mean. For the purposes of the multistate theory, the final meaning listed above is the one I suggest replacing with *mindbody.* This will help avoid the ambiguity of *consciousness* and emphasize overall patterns of mind + body functioning, where body and mind are not seen as two related things but rather as one, combined, unified whole.

Whatever meaning you attach to consciousness, you can ask: How does consciousness vary from mindbody state to mindbody state?

Mindapps and Metaintelligence

The second major concept in the multistate theory, which I have termed *mindapp,* can be regarded as a synonym for the more heavy-duty word *psychotechnology* or *psychological agents of transformation.* Of the words and phrases that I've coined, *mindapp* is my favorite; when you understand the idea behind it, all the other words and phrases fall into place. I also chose *mindapp* because it offers a fertile analogy for thinking about our minds:

Apps are to devices
as
mindapps are to minds.

That is, mindapps function analogously to the way programs and apps function in electronic devices. This analogy does not mean that our brains are merely biological computers. I particularly like mindapps because it produces two fruitful ideas: just as digital apps extend the power of our devices, mindapps extend the power of our minds, and just as we can write and install a large number of apps in our digital devices, we can design and install a large number mindapps in our brain-mind complex. If you remember only one idea from this book, make it *mindapps*.

Mindapps → Metaintelligence

By one definition, mindapps increase intelligence: cognitive psychologist Robert Sternberg defined intelligence as **"mental self-management."**[16] Thus, as we increase the repertoire of our mental abilities by installing more mindapps, we increase our intelligence. The authors of "Connectome-Harmonic Decomposition of Human Brain Activity Reveals Dynamical Repertoire Re-organization under LSD" say, "These results demonstrate that the **increased power and energy of brain states** activity under LSD is caused by both an extended repertoire of active brain states over time as well as increased activity of certain states."[17]

From a singlestate perspective, intelligence is the ability to use our default state skillfully. From a multistate perspective, intelligence expands to include the ability to select mindbody states and to use their useful resident abilities. In 2006, I named the ability to select the appropriate mindbody state for the task at hand *metaintelligence*.[18]

A Mindapp Population Boom

Usually when we think of technologies, we think of electronic, biological, or mechanical technologies. **Mindapps**[19] are currently an under-recognized class of biotechnologies, which install mindbody states. Among mindapps are families of selected exercise routines, meditation, psychoactive plants and chemicals, yoga and the martial arts, sensory overload and sensory deprivation, hypnosis and receptive relaxation, sleep and sleep deprivation, chanting, dream work, breathing techniques, biofeedback and neurofeedback, transcranial magnetic stimulation, biohacking, CRISPER and other genetic techniques, contemplative prayer, vision quests and rites of passage, selected practices in Eastern and indigenous religions, drumming, and many (perhaps thousands) more. Furthermore, each of those listed here is not just one, lone mindapp but rather a whole family of related mindapps, such as the many types of meditation and contemplative prayer. They all contribute to the multistate theory.

A fertile source of potential future mindapps are the almost daily discoveries about our brains. While current brain research is primarily done to discover treatments for diseases and conditions, some—if not all—such discoveries have the potential to develop into new mindapps too, although brain researchers seldom point to these additional benefits. I find **Mind & Brain News,**[20] a free online service of *ScienceDaily,* a fascinating way to keep up, and it's written for nonspecialists.

Globalization is another source of potential mindapps. The import and export of mindapps is increasing our repertoire of mindapps and the mindbody states they install, for example, ayahuasca, ibogaine, and imported spiritual practices.

The list of psychoactive drugs reaches well into the hundreds. Similarly, lists of all kinds of meditation or of the many martial arts would quickly exceed dozens and perhaps even hundreds. I suppose a full census of mindapps would reach into the thousands and remains a task to be accomplished.

Mindapps as Research Variables

Thanks to a mindapps angle, a number of traditional and new topics open up to fresh perspectives.

- A full map of the human mind needs to include all mindbody states, all their resident functions, and all the mindapps for achieving them.

- A typology of mindapps and their respective mindbody states should also characterize states; this remains a task for students of mind studies: How many different states are there and how are their abilities linked? When and how do some mindapps blend into others, for example, when do relaxation, guided imagery, and meditation blend into each other?
- By following shifts in one ability, say, logical reasoning, can we characterize, notice, and track mindbody shifts?
- To what extent is it possible to transfer knowledge or a skill from one state to another? Remembering dreams is a common example.
- How many different ways will it be useful to differentiate one mindbody state from another? Will stipulations vary to fit the fields of research and questions being asked?

In determining where one state ends and another begins, the way we approach the light spectrum is a useful analogy; we can simply stipulate the border between red and orange at a certain frequency. However, the number of things (parameters) that make up a mindbody state is huge, much more vast than a simple electromagnetic frequency, so what we decide to pay most attention to is likely to change depending on what topic we're looking at.

As we characterize mindbody states, we are likely to stumble onto surprising new, unexpected parameters. For example, when he looked at **how cognitive psychology and ayahuasca can inform each other,**[21] Benny Shanon, a professor of cognitive sciences at Hebrew University, to his surprise, ran across a dozen unexpected experiences, such as being oneself at the same time as being something else, consciousness located outside oneself, and more. These weren't included in traditional singlestate cognitive studies. In the section "A Systematic Method for Inventing Paradigms?" of chapter 4, we'll look at these discoveries as clues for how to expand current paradigms and how to invent new ones. How many unexpected parameters will our growing number of mindapps produce in our growing set of mindbody states? How will we judge what does or doesn't qualify as a new parameter?

Residence and the Central Multistate Question

The third major concept in the multistate theory is *residence*. Our mindbody states produce or house all our mental and physical capacities, experiences, and behaviors; that is, all our capacities reside in— are expressions of—their respective mindbody states. We can think of mindbody states as the programs whose outputs are everything we do: each state has its distinctive repertoire of outputs. As we move from one state to another, some of our capacities become stronger and others weaker. In addition to strength, other varieties of default-state capacities may exist in other states. Recovery of memories in psychotherapeutic states is an example.

As we explore additional **mindbody states, anomalies**[22] are likely to occur, and some of the things we now call "impossible" may seem that way only because we've looked for them only in our default state.

While residence reframes the disciplines that singlestate scientists and humanists are used to, the central multistate question plants seed-questions for vast new realms of "**normal puzzle solving**,"[23] as Kuhn named it.

The central multistate question is *How does/do _____ vary from mindbody state to mindbody state?*

To sample the opportunities that the central multistate question and its theory offer, try inserting the topics below into the question above.

philosophy	thinking	I
cognition	consciousness	logic
meaning	learning	memory
language	aesthetics	theology
truth	emotions	perception
performance	mind	observation
values	identity	reason

To invent additional hypotheses, questions, and intellectual agendas, insert your favorite topics. We can insert every topic we wonder about into this question, then explore the topic in all mindapps. The result? An overwhelming explosion of creative questions, hypotheses, topics, observations, professional agendas, and even mindbody methods of investigating them.

Current psychedelic clinical research partially answers the question "How does healing vary from mindbody state to mindbody state?" Questions such as "How does consciousness arise?" are better studied from wider databases, and every mindapp adds another instance and key to characterizing the human mind. The mindapp line of questioning is endless. I find these three broad questions especially intriguing:

- Given that positive emotions boost the immune system and that mystical experiences provide intense positive emotions, **"Do psychedelic-induced mystical experiences boost the immune system?"**[24]

- How does the default mode network vary from mindbody state to mindbody state? The default mode network is a large-scale brain network of interacting brain regions that are highly correlated with each other and distinct from other networks in the brain. It is especially active when thinking about oneself, social relations, and the past and future.

- What mindapps, if any, activate the brain terminals of the vagus nerves? The vagus nerves are responsible for communicating from our brains to our throat, lungs, heart, and abdominal organs and back again. What bodily effects result?

Adventurous scholars can enter various mindbody states and do their scholarly work within them or informed by them afterward. Chapter 4 explores this idea more fully. Our minds can become experimental variables. Psychedelics and other mindapps can all become both *objects* of study and *methods* of study. It's clear that the multistate theory promotes a fuller view of our minds, generates useful ideas, and releases a flood of research questions, but so far we've looked at mindapps only one at a time. What happens if we combine several of them together, say, as ingredients in any number of possible mindbody recipes? In the next chapter, we'll visit a still stranger approach—more distinctive, more demanding, certainly more extraordinary.

How might these acorn ideas grow to mighty oaks?

Centers for Mindapp Research and Development

3
Mind Design
Mindapps → Artificial Intelligence in the Brain-Mind Complex

The idea of mindapps is the most fertile idea in this book; mind design is the most adventurous. For intellectual adventurers who take pleasure in exploring new directions, a far vaster horizon beckons—designing new mindbody states, artificial ones that have never existed before. From a broad perspective, what is now informally under way is another form of artificial intelligence—*mindappAI*—one based not on digital information processing but on brain-mind information processing in newly invented "artificial" mindbody states. Is this a misuse of the expression *AI* as it is currently used? I see *mindappAI* as honoring *artificial intelligence* of the digital world and borrowing it to denote designed, constructed, artificial mindbody states. In addition to trying to digitally emulate the most productive information-processing system we know of—our brains—why not simply start with them and add to their repertoires? Model *and* augment. Digital AI and mindappAI complement each other.

ENDLESS MINDAPPAI RECIPES

MindappAI—synthesizing new mindbody states and developing them—fits within existing scientific frontiers and the history of science: physicists have created synthetic elements; chemists invented synthetic molecules, and synthetic biology is taking off. It is time for psychologists and other mind designers to combine mindapps into new recipes of two, three, or more mindapp ingredients, to synthesize new mindbody states, detail their characteristics, and research and develop their putative resident abilities.

In my opinion, this is today's biggest intellectual opportunity; mindappAI offers new ways to study the human mind, new ways to use it in research, and opportunities to design our minds' futures. New mindbody states boost all the questions emanating from the central multistate question and are joined by a rank of new ones.

SELECTED MINDAPPAI QUESTIONS

- Will mindapps and the multistate theory encourage adventurous mind designers to compose novel mindbody states?
- Who dares to discover what various combinations of, say, psychedelics + neurofeedback + transcranial magnetic stimulation will produce? The possible recipes run into the hundreds of thousands.
- When we explore new mindbody states, will we discover new abilities that reside in them?
- Is a complete map of the human mind impossible? Such a map would have to include our minds in their fullest mindbody ramifications. In the future new mindbody states will continue to flower, so the map will flower too. The same is true for virtual models.

- What does it mean to have the experimenter's mind itself an experimental variable?
- Do scholars, scientists, and others have the intellectual courage to personally explore new geographies of the mind?
- If, as Lotem et al. claim, "We believe that, over lengthy time scales, some aspects of the **brain must have changed** to better accommodate the learning parameters required by various cultural activities,"[1] will human brains adapt to a multistate culture?

MindappAI recipes demand questions that are novel, complex, and challenging; these and similar questions point researchers to the richest intellectual opportunities of our time. They also lead us to complex social and professional policy issues.

Whoa! While a standard **best practices model**[2] is emerging for psychotherapy—careful screening, hours of preparation, session monitoring, integration, and follow-up—it is not at all clear what their best-practice counterparts will be for the use of psychedelics for entheogenic, intellectual, and ideagenic uses. Before institutions and individual researchers jump in head first, these **problems of policy and practice**[3] need to be explored and tentatively settled. Nevertheless, in spite of this caution, as creative people invent new mindapps and combine them into artificial mindbody states, the future of the human mind is infinite.

Precautions aside, it's hard to pretend that our students and colleagues are not already psychedelic researchers, and many have been so for many years. For example, in 1998 at a meeting of **the Serotonin Club**[4]* at the annual meeting of the Society for Neuroscience, Dave Nichols began his talk, "Let me start off by suggesting that a significant number of the people in this room tonight and indeed a significant percentage of serotonin researchers worldwide first gained

---

*Serotonin is a neurotransmitter whose structure closely resembles that of LSD. Since Dr. Nichols's talk in 1998, the club has evolved into the International Society for Serotonin Research.

their interest in serotonin through some association with psychedelic agents." Professional curiosity trumps social strictures.

As Kuhn wrote, to historians of science it looks like "**when paradigms change**, the world changes with them. Led by a new paradigm, scientists adopt new instruments [mindapps] and look in new places [mindbody states]. Even more important, during revolutions [neuro]scientists see new and different things when looking with familiar instruments in places they have looked before."[5]

How do we move these ideas into action?

Foundation for Mind Design

4
Mindapps
for the Sciences

In the previous chapters, we saw some questions that mindapps may elicit. While some disciplines may address these specific questions both empirically and theoretically, used individually and in combination, mindapps reformulate scientific perspectives on some broader fundamental topics.

EXPERIMENTAL APPROACHES
TO SCIENTIFIC CONCEPTS

Before psychedelics, researching some higher-level scientific concepts was mainly restricted to armchair musing; now the multistate theory encourages us to reconsider them—even to design experiments on some concepts such as consilience, emergence, and the "hard problem."

Consilience
Naming his 1998 book after its main idea, E. O. Wilson proposed "**consilience**,"[1] a hoped-for model of the sciences that could combine them into one overall scaffolding "by the linking of facts and fact-based theory across disciplines to create a common groundwork of explana-

tion." One way to advance his project is to link disciplines by having an independent variable in one discipline and the dependent in another. Enough such studies will braid disciplines together. "The strategy that works best in these enterprises is the construction of coherent cause-and-effect explanations across levels of organization," and this goes beyond the scientific disciplines, **"to unite the natural sciences with the social sciences and humanities."**[2]

Psychedelics and other mindapps are ready-made for this project, as Wilson recognized. He cited the use of **ayahuasca as a clue**[3] to how explanation "in some instances can be achieved across all levels of organization and hence all branches of learning." Writing about how the psychoactive plants of the Amazon produce psychological and social effects, he recognized that "the sacred plants, which have been analyzed by chemists, are no longer mysterious. Their juices are laced with neuromodulators that in large oral doses produce excitation, delirium, and visions." Science, working in concert with anthropology? As this century's **experiments in medical schools**[4] show too, the biochemical psilocybin input yields cognitive, spiritual, aesthetic, social, and other higher-level outputs, proving that science and the humanities need not work separately. Psychedelics researchers, please take note: your work contains hidden nuggets that inform consilience.

Emergence

This leads to the most difficult and fascinating of hard questions. When things are put together, new, unexpected characteristics appear that the individual components didn't previously show. Water is the most common example. Hydrogen gas and oxygen gas each have their characteristics, but when they are combined into water, the so-called watery qualities emerge anew. How? Why? A common assumption about our minds and their mental properties is that they emerge from our brains. However mind emergence occurs, it will help us understand this process if we have additional samples, and a variety of mindbody states will produce them. Creating new instances of mind emergence will add to our sample size: this is an opportunity to found the field of experimental emergence studies.

The Hard Problem and the Harder (Impossible?) Problem

When we approach emergence from a multistate perspective, we find not only a way to approach what's known as "the hard problem" but also a way to formulate what may be "the hardest problem," even, perhaps, "the impossible problem." David Chalmers posed what he named "**the hard problem.**"[5] He said, "The really hard problem of consciousness is the problem of experience. . . . It is widely agreed that experience arises from a physical basis, but we have no good explanation of why and how it so arises. Why should physical processing give rise to a rich inner life at all?" To address the hard problem, it would be handy to have additional instances of it, of how brain produces consciousness. Mindapps, particularly psychedelics, provide such instances.

This "hard problem" of body-to-mind emergence leads us to a still harder one. I'm tempted to call it "the impossible problem"—*Are there general laws of emergence?*—that is, are there laws that hold, not just for when oxygen and hydrogen form water and when brain produces mind, but up and down the full spectrum of theory and observations from subatomic to abstract conceptualization or to (who knows what the highest level is?)? This problem is so fascinating, important, complex, and especially difficult that I do not expect philosophers and scientists to make any progress on this topic in the foreseeable future. I hope I am wrong.

Also, when previously separate parts combine into a larger whole, they lose some of their previous characteristics. For example, when hydrogen and oxygen gases combine to form water, they lose their gaseous characteristics. Perhaps we should call this "demergence."

A SYSTEMATIC METHOD
FOR INVENTING PARADIGMS?

Some assumptions that are constant in singlestate psychology change in multistate psychology. Explicit examples come from **Benny Shanon's work with ayahuasca.**[6] A cognitive psychologist from Israel, he ran across ayahuasca while on vacation in Brazil and became intrigued with how cognition changed with this psychedelic. Ordinary, singlestate cognitive concepts didn't fit his own experiences or those of the many South Americans, North Americans, and Europeans he interviewed. He identified eleven experiences that point to **changes in thinking that singlestate mind studies miss**[7] or can't account for. Here are three:

- Personal identity—personal identification with whatever one is looking at, a sense of unity with the other
- Unity—being oneself at the same time as being someone or something else
- Self-consciousness—a "residue" of the normal self after other factors of consciousness have completely disappeared

In *Antipodes,* he identifies a new method of cognitive studies that should be adapted across the intellectual spectrum.

> The bringing together of Ayahuasca research and cognitive psychology defines **a two-way interaction.** Not only can a cognitive-psychological analysis make a crucial contribution to the study of Ayahuasca, the converse is also the case—the study of Ayahuasca may have implications of import to our general understanding of the workings of the human mind.[8]

Has Shanon stumbled onto a multistate method for constructing new paradigms, one that will be useful across the intellectual spectrum? Failure to explore these possible agendas is intellectual cowardice.

A STANDARD FOR JUDGING EMPIRICAL FINDINGS AND THEORETICAL CLAIMS

Multistate theory also provides a standard for judging the strength of empirical findings and generalizations. A general rule in research is that the more diverse a database, the stronger are the findings derived from it. While not falling into the trap of the singlestate fallacy, current research on meditation, hypnosis, dreams, and other mindbody states, including our default state, generally derives its data sets, theories, and generalizations from only one state. Identifying which findings hold across several mindbody states and which are state-specific will help develop a more complex and complete map of the mind and its processes. I would trust the findings of multistate scholars more than those of their singlestate colleagues.

Investigating Impossibilities

Generally when we say that a specific human behavior or experience is possible or impossible, we are implying but seldom acknowledging that we mean "in our ordinary awake, default state." Rare and unusual abilities and even some so-called impossible abilities and events may seem impossible to us because we have looked for them only in our default state. As we systematically examine other mindbody states using normal science, however, as Kuhn might predict, we are likely to find **anomalous**[9] perceptions, skills, and abilities that don't reside in our default mindbody state. One of the most common psychedelic anomalies is synesthesia, for example, when words and letters appear in colors.

Reports of **synesthesia**[10] with psychedelics are not unusual. However, in 2017 when Terhune, Luke, and Cohen surveyed the literature, they said that it precluded them from "making firm conclusions regarding whether chemical agents can induce genuine synaesthesia." In 2018, a team led by Nichols combined electroencephalography and transcranial magnetic stimulation **to teach synesthesia**[11] and measured its underlying brain plasticity. Conflicting findings like these cry for further research, say, by combining these mindapps.

The psychedelic jungles are rich places for anomaly hunting. Grof's patients reported **birth memories and transpersonal experiences.**[12] Stretching anomalies further, David Luke's *Otherworlds: **Psychedelics and Exceptional Human Experience***[13] discusses synesthesia, extra-dimensional percepts, interspecies communication, eco-consciousness, mediumship, possession, entity encounters, near-death and out-of-body experiences, psi, alien abduction experiences, and lycanthropy. Combined with the startling psychotherapeutic results that psychedelics originally produced, will these produce enough anomalies to invoke the **crises**[14] that are "a necessary precondition of novel theories"?

At least, investigating them further will allow us to decide which are subjective experiences only and which are early sightings that extend our view of reality. In addition to expanding theory to encompass anomalous reports and challenging them to experimentation, at the very least, such explorations will allow us to characterize unusual subjective experiences more fully and map the fascinating ambivalent gray areas where subjective reports and empirical observations overlap.

Standing in meta-positions behind specific disciplinary thinking, psychedelics, and all mindapps, allow experimental approaches to foundational, broad-based meta-topics. Going even deeper, psychedelics in particular can improve researchers' minds.

IMPROVING RESEARCHERS' MINDS

"Each discipline has its tools, and each such tool has its own inherent errors," wrote Lawrence Kubie more than sixty years ago. And, he continued, "A discipline comes of age and a student of that discipline reaches maturity when it becomes possible to recognize, estimate, and allow for the errors of their tools." So far so good. "Yet there is **one instrument which every discipline uses** without checking its errors, tacitly assuming that the instrument is error-free. This, of course, is the human psychological apparatus."[15] That is, as omnipresent research instruments, intellectuals' minds need tune-ups too. Scientists who believe in the value of experimental evidence should welcome their own minds becoming experimental variables. I do not understand how one can pretend to be objective or critical without being objective and critical of one's own cognitive processes.

While Kubie is warning us against unconscious mental interference from emotional events in our developmental history, psychedelics might help us compensate for them with moderate-dose psycholytic therapy (therapy that loosens the mind and brings unconscious thoughts to light). As Yensen and Dryer wrote, "(Grof 1975) holds that the effects of these drugs on consciousness resemble those of an amplifier or catalyst for the unconscious. With this analogy he introduces the use of psychedelics as tools for the observation of psychological processes. His research attempts to understand the dynamics of the unconscious mind, using LSD as an **amplifier of unconscious mental processes**,"[16] thus helping researchers adjust for their unconscious biases.

All the instances of psycholytic, moderate-dose exploration that I know of examined people's emotional and social lives for psychotherapeutic benefits. With the exception of Shanon (above), I know of no cases that focus on the intellectual side of life. We simply don't know what insights might occur if intellectuals used moderate doses to examine their disciplines, specialties, their own work and ideas, colleagues, intellectual contexts, and so forth. Can moderate psychedelic doses inform intellectual lives as they have social-emotional lives?

Kubie's warning is doubly apt for psychedelicists; the sometimes overwhelming sense of truthful insight during sessions makes us susceptible to unbridled enthusiasm for our own ideas, as the internet bears witness too often. Psychedelic states, like our default mindbody state, generate both valuable and worthless ideas.

Open-Mindedness

Judging from my own experience and that of my professional colleagues, a curious side-effect of psychedelics is becoming more at ease with anomalies: not blindly willing to accept any odd event, but not feeling threatened by them either. The psilocybin experiments at Johns Hopkins Medical School raise fascinating issues about the personality trait of open-mindedness. When people had mystical experiences via psilocybin in an established protocol, their **open-mindedness increased**[17] as measured by a **standard personality instrument.**[18] This was surprising: "There is general agreement that **personality traits are relatively enduring** styles of thinking, feeling, and acting."[19] They are usually set for life when people are in their midtwenties or early thirties; yet, the average age of the hallucinogen-naive volunteers was forty-six. How would today's middle-aged scholars react? Can psychedelics become a teaching tool—illegal for now of course—to help professors remain fresh, to help students learn this valuable intellectual skill, and to help citizens learn an important civic attitude? In the meantime, meditation and other mindapps offer legal opportunities for expanding one's personality.

From a multistate perspective, skillful thinking requires skillful thinkers to use both a range of ideas in our default state and a range of cognitive processes from a variety of mindbody states. This requires a radical shift from singlestate to multistate thinking.

ENHANCING SCHOLARLY COGNITION

Current discussions of cognitive enhancement almost all have to do with discovering ways to boost our default state's current cognitive skills. A multistate perspective offers wider perspectives.

Creative Problem-Solving

In 1966, Harman, McKim, Mogar, Fadiman, and Stolaroff investigated the question, "Can the psychedelic experience [mescaline] **enhance** creative problem-solving ability,[20] and if so, what is the concrete evidence of enhancement?"[21] Their answer was "Yes." The evidence? From business and academic backgrounds, twenty-seven psychedelic-naive professionals solved forty-four professional problems that they had previously worked on unsuccessfully. With psychologist Howard Gardner defining *intelligence* as "the ability to solve problems or produce goods of value within one or more cultural settings,"[22] this mescaline study meets that criterion. The benefits continued: "Many subjects in the follow-up interviews reported changes in their working behaviors consistent with the enhancement experienced during the session itself." In my opinion, this lead is the hottest one in promising long-term benefits to humanity. What field wouldn't advance faster if it had improved problem-solving skills?

Microdosing

Half a century later, a grandchild of this study is **microdosing**.[23] This entails taking very small doses, usually ten to twenty micrograms every three or four days, to increase one's ordinary functioning. Microdosing is one of the hot topics among young **businesspeople and technology professionals**,[24] but it has not been scientifically researched. Would microdosing be productive in academia too?

Connectome Intelligence—Better Connected Brains?

Three articles raise a fascinating possibility. Briefly stated, psychedelics → augmented **connectome** (the brain's internal wiring)[25] → higher IQ. The first, from Imperial College, shows that psilocybin **adds communication networks within human brains**[26] that are not usually connected. That is, it adds "wiring," so to speak, to the brain's internal wiring system, to its *connectome*. In figure 4.1 on page 53, the small circles on the perimeters represent parts of the brain; the curved lines show connections between them. The circle on the left shows connections in the brain under normal conditions; the circle on the right shows the connections with psilocybin. The number of possible

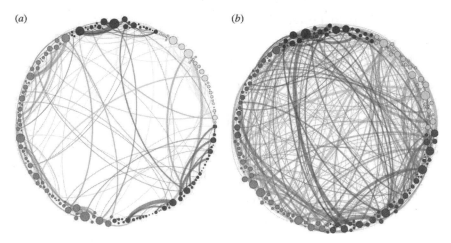

*Fig. 4.1. Intra-brain connections. The circle on the right
shows connections with psilocybin.*

connections, the parts of the brain, are the same in each circle. On the
right, the connections go between more places; while on the left they
link along well-used, heavy pathways. Thus, it is not the number of
possible connections that is different but rather the number of different communication links.

From my perspective, the addition of communication networks
in the brain is one of the most provocative findings in current brain
research. Multistate theory asks: What diagrams might other mindapps
produce? What about combinations of mindapps?

The second article, "Smart People Have Better Connected Brains,"
from Goethe University, reports that "certain brain regions are more
strongly involved in the **flow of information between brain regions.**"[27]
The article also cautions against attributing too much to the impact of
psilocybin: "However, it is equally as likely that the frequent use of the
brain for **cognitively challenging** tasks may positively influence the
development of brain networks."[28] Without a doubt, psychedelics and
other mindapps provide "challenging cognitive tasks," so the improvement may be due to increased connections, cognitively demanding
tasks, or a combination. Presumably moving among mindbody states

is cognitively demanding, so increased IQ may occur with transitions among other mindbody states too.

The third article, from the University of Cambridge, reported a new **brain imaging and mapping technique**[29] that highlights the **relationship between connectivity and IQ.**[30] "We saw a clear link between the 'hubbiness' of higher-order brain regions—how densely connected they were to the rest of the network—and an individual's IQ," said Jacob Seidlitz, the chief author. He added, "This makes sense if you think of the hubs as enabling the flow of information around the brain—the stronger the connections, the better the brain is at processing information."

Are these coincidences, or do these three pieces of a psychedelic-connectome-IQ puzzle fit together? Do psychedelics increase connections that raise IQ? Like most psychedelic research, the answer will probably be "some of the time under the right conditions." An additional opportunity opens the door to a wider brain-mind possibility: if psychedelics can establish original links among useful parts of our brains, can those links also be strengthened by, say, neurofeedback, transcranial brain stimulation, meditation, and other mindapps?

This lead ought to be followed. Should psychedelic researchers experiment on themselves? If they believe their work contributes to their disciplines or to broader human welfare, isn't it a moral and professional duty to develop their minds' highest capacities to perform these benefits? Also, scholars who study the human mind without including the observations to which they have privileged access—their own minds—are denying a distinctive source of data.

RHEOSTATS OF THE MIND? EXPERIMENTAL INTENSITY?

"This is realer than real . . . the ultimate truth . . . the most meaningful experience possible . . . sacred beyond belief . . . profoundly portentous . . . deeply insightful . . . more beautiful than I thought possible"—these and similar expressions of exceptional intensity are common expressions from people who have had powerful experiences, especially mystical ones. A sense of impending, profoundly significant portent is the scent I've been tracking since my first LSD experience in 1970; for me, it stands behind the others, is their foundation, and empowers the feelings of truth, sacredness, beauty, and so on. I suppose that for other people, sacredness, truth, beauty, and so on are their foundations, and I suppose they construct their default states' primary orientations to the world.

Considering psychedelics' "ability to amplify perception of meaning," Ido Hartogshon, now a scholar at Bar Ilan University in Israel, proposed "that the tendency of these agents to enhance the **perception of significance** offers valuable clues to explaining their reported ability to stimulate a variety of therapeutic processes, enhance creativity, and instigate mystical-type experiences."[31] The perception of significance refers to how powerful a stimulus feels, whether it is underwhelming, "normal," overwhelming, or somewhere between these set thresholds. Psychedelics can turn the "volume" of an experience up or down.

What are we to make of this? Now, thanks to psychedelics, we can experiment—repeat, can experiment—with increasing and decreasing the intensity of what we feel about our thoughts, our feelings, our sensations, our perceptions, and our values. Subjectively, it's as if there were, so to say, rheostats in the mind, and we can move them up and down. Or, perhaps some ideas produce a sort of cognitive qualia (essential quality), similar to perceptual qualia, and we can similarly perceive them with greater or lesser strength. However we approach this intellectual puzzle box, psychedelics and their mindapp cousins provide an experimental way to study the subjective feeling of intensity in its many manifestations.

GRADUATE RESEARCH METHODS

Inside current fields of inquiry, the central multistate question releases a tidal flood of normal science questions, and anomalies analogous to those that Benny Shanon found, and they are also grounds for critiquing our current disciplines. Will visionary graduate programs instruct their students on how to enter the mindbody states where psychedelic insights reside? Outside our current fields of inquiry, more profound—and certainly more speculative—opportunities come from using all mindapps and the mindbody states they produce.

Systematic exploration of the full range of mindbody states, characterizing them and their resident abilities, are huge projects that remain in the quest to describe and develop our minds fully. Elsewhere, I called it **"The Neurosingularity Project."**[32] The Neurosingularity Project is the discovery, construction, description, and development of useful abilities in all mindbody states, both natural and synthetic. It posits a time when our future mindbody states will surpass today's.

Besides asking new ranges of normal science questions, releasing a flood of central multistate questions, inventing paradigms, and increasing problem-solving ability, mindapps allow us to experimentally approach some of science's underlying concepts, such as consilience and emergence, all the while improving scientists' thinking processes. As we'll see in the next chapters, parallel advances enrich nonscientific topics as well.

How do we move these ideas into action?

Conference Sessions: Scientists' Minds as Experimental Variables

5
Layers of Meaning
Riding Grof's Bathyscaphe
into Our Minds

This unique property of psychedelics makes it possible to study **psychological undercurrents that govern our experiences**[1] *and behaviors to a depth that cannot be matched by any other method or tool available in mainstream psychiatry or psychology.*

STANISLAV GROF

And I have found so much of my thinking about mythic forms freshly illuminated by the findings here reported that I am going to try in the last few pages to render a suggestion of the types of consciousness that Dr. Grof has fathomed in his search of our inward sea.

JOSEPH CAMPBELL

When researchers working independently and unknown to each other reach the same conclusion, that result gains credibility. In the work of Stanislav Grof, psychedelics offer corroboration from and to religion, psychiatry, and mythology. His ideas, corroborated by others, offer a new map for exploration of these topics and more.

BATHYSCAPHE TO THE DEPTHS
OF OUR INNER SEA

In addition to coining the term *transpersonal,* helping to found the Transpersonal Institute, serving on the editorial board of *The Journal of Transpersonal Psychology,* and as first president of the International Transpersonal Association, Grof's decades of clinical experience, extensive list of publications, and numerous lectures and workshops **carried psychedelics forward during years of neglect and oppression.**[2]

Grof's psychedelic clinical therapy produced two forms of psychedelic psychotherapy: psycholytic and peak experience. In the former, a moderate dose brings unconscious materials to consciousness; then the therapist and patient work through it, taking as many non-dose sessions as necessary. While doing **low-dose, or *psycholytic,***[3] LSD clinical research in Prague, he discovered to his own surprise that some of his patients remembered their own births, and others even had transpersonal experiences during their therapeutic sessions. His map of the human mind is derived from these sessions.

Later at the Maryland Psychiatric Research Institute, he and his research team developed **high-dose peak-experience psychedelic psychotherapy.**[4] "It was developed on the basis of dramatic clinical improvements and profound personality changes observed in LSD subjects whose sessions had a very definite religious or mystical emphasis." This new direction honed the treatment protocol to include the precursors of **methods that are generally used today,**[5] for example, at the Johns Hopkins Medical School's Behavior Pharmacology Research Unit: careful screening, establishing patient-therapist rapport, music, blindfolds, a relaxed setting, a co-therapist team, and post-session follow-up and integration.

Grof's research and that of his successors is proof of concept, showing that it is possible to gain new perspectives via experimental research on topics such as mind, meaningfulness, spirituality, sacredness, beauty, mystical experiences, well-being, altruism, sense of self, ego transcendence, archetypes, ancestral memories, creativity, and noetic knowing. In addition to these specific topics, **Grof's four-level map of our minds**[6] (especially its perinatal level) and his pioneering psychedelic findings detail our view of the human mind. My reason for mentioning this is not to summarize the model nor to portray its powerful psychotherapeutic values, but primarily to point out how this theory is culturally fruitful.

GROF'S FOUR-LEVEL MODEL

Psychedelics amplify or magnify one's awareness of subjective human experiences, both emotional and cognitive. Although not originally intended for that reason, clinical sessions commonly manifest cultural allusions, not only from a patient's own background but also, most puzzlingly, from unknown sources. This is rich hunting ground for the humanities and social sciences. Using LSD as a sort of microscope to examine the mind, Grof conducted more than four thousand psychoanalytic sessions and later reviewed records of several thousand additional sessions; thus, his sampling of the human mind is immense. In *Higher Wisdom,* psychiatrists Roger Walsh and Charles Grob evaluated Grof's knowledge of the human mind: "He has therefore perhaps seen a **vaster panoply of human experience** than anyone else in history."[7] Just as the microscope benefited biology and medicine by allowing scientists to assemble hundreds of individual magnified close-ups into detailed pictures of the human body—for example, a microscopic atlas of the liver—Grof has pieced together a psychedelics-based atlas of the human mind. This map also moves our understanding of the human mind forward by integrating psychedelics' perceptual richness, the biographical memories of Freudian-psychodynamic psychology, Otto Rank's ideas regarding "birth trauma," and Jung's adventures into the collective unconscious. Grof's map integrates these into one overall model.

Using the Freudian figurative trope of the mind having depth, Grof arranged his map of the mind into layers going from the shallowest (at the top of the map) to the deepest (at the bottom of the map).

Abstract and aesthetic: thoughts and perceptions

Psychodynamic: biographical, personal history from birth to the present

Perinatal: prenatal and birth memories—often physical rather than cognitive

Transpersonal: experiences going beyond self-identity, time, and space

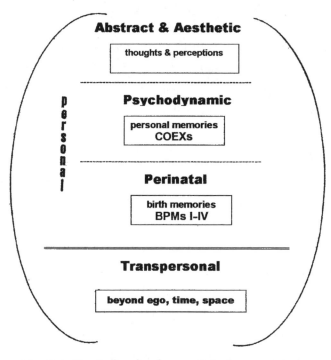

Fig. 5.1. Grof's four-level map of the human mind.
A COEX is a constellation of experiences, memories, and fantasies that cluster together along a common theme (negative ones such as anxieties, depressions, and fears or positive ones such as pride, achievement, and love). Grof says that they are the major structures in the autobiographical layer of our minds. BPMs (Basic Perinatal Matrices) have the same functions in our mind's birth level. They are described in more detail on page 63.

APPLYING GROF'S MODEL

Psychology, religion, mythology, philosophy—when scholars following different lines of thought converge on the same conclusion, their findings are immensely stronger than when researchers following the same line agree.

Religious Studies

In *Forgotten Truth: The Primordial Tradition,* Huston Smith noted a correspondence among Grof's four-level map of the human mind and "the **outlooks of tribes, societies, civilizations,** and at deepest levels the world's great religions—these collective outlooks admit of one overview. What then emerges is a remarkable unity underlying the surface variety."[8] After describing this unity as the main theme of the book, in an appendix Smith evaluated Grof's clinical research in light of his own theory of "what the mind is." He wrote, "Judged both by quantity of data encompassed and by the explanatory power of the hypotheses that make sense of this data, it is **the most formidable evidence the psychedelics have thus far produced.**"[9] He added, "The view of **reality that results is so uncannily** like the one that has been outlined in this book that, interlacing paraphrases of passages from Grof's article with direct quotations from it, we present here in summary."[10] Smith continued his interlacing for two pages.

In *Cleansing the Doors of Perception,* Smith updated a collection of his earlier papers plus some new ones and reiterated his view that the entheogenic uses of psychedelics enrich our understanding of religion. Thus, to Grof's finding that later stages in the LSD sequence conform sufficiently to the stages of the birth process to warrant our saying that **they [religions] are influenced by those stages,**[11] tradition adds: "influenced by" only, not caused by.

A vast literature—some Grofian, most not—examined relationships between spiritual development and the entheogenic uses of psychedelics.

As chapter 8 of this book describes, the **entheogenic field of inquiry**[12] is growing with increasing speed and even points to a possible future of experimental religious studies.

Mythology

Joseph Campbell, compiling much of the world's mythology, and Grof, excavating the human mind, found that their studies independently corroborated each other's work. After he received an early manuscript of Grof's key book ***Realms of the Human Unconscious,***[13] Campbell wrote as quoted above that much of his thinking about mythic forms had been freshly illuminated. He decided to try "to render a suggestion of the types and depths of consciousness that Dr. Grof has fathomed in his **search of our inward sea.**"[14] After taking more than three pages noting parallels between Grof's perinatal level and images from folk myth and the world's religions, Campbell summarized, "**It is these [perinatal stages] that are represented in myth.** As illustrated in the various mythologies of the peoples of the world, however, the universals have been everywhere localized to the sociopolitical context."[15]

Campbell, of course, is widely known as the author of *The Hero with a Thousand Faces,* in which he claimed that a common theme runs through major legends, myths, and religions. "**The passage of the mythological hero** may be over-ground, incidentally; fundamentally it is inward—into depths where obscure resistances are overcome, and long lost, forgotten powers are revivified, to be made available for the transfiguration of the world."[16] This could just as well describe psychedelic journeys.

The Consciousness Explorer as Hero

Psychedelics in the late twentieth century and early twenty-first century give us another new face for today's heroes—the consciousness explorer as hero. Judging from the honor and excitement they arouse, the heroes in the psychedelic line of consciousness explorers include Albert Hofmann, Ronald Sandison, R. D. Laing, Stanislav Grof, Humphry

Osmond, Timothy Leary, Ram Dass, Ralph Metzner, Aldous Huxley, Terence McKenna, John Lilly, R. Gordon Wasson, James Fadiman, Walter Pahnke, Al Hubbard, Ken Kesey, Richard Schultes, Maria Sabina, Jean Houston and Robert Masters, Sasha and Ann Shulgin, Owsley, Leo Zeff . . . the list goes on and on to include more of the quick and the dead.

In addition to these elders, we might add many others in today's laboratories, hospitals, clinics, universities, and organizations as well as musicians and other artists. Some in this list are already cultural heroes among psychedelicists, as shown by their almost legendary status. They have, as Campbell described, traveled "beneath the floor of the comparatively neat little dwelling that we call our consciousness" and actively explored the "**adventure of the discovery of the self.**"[17]

Perinatal Level Analysis

Judging by the number of publications, Grof's third level, the perinatal, has been the most fruitful, revealing a hidden pattern that clarifies our idea of mind and charts its cultural expressions.

In skeletal form, the perinatal level contains four stages that parallel the birth process.

BPM = BASIC PERINATAL MATRIX,
A COMPLEX OF EMOTIONS AND
PHYSICAL EXPERIENCES

BPM I = relaxed, satisfied womb experiences; usually blissful.

BPM II = being trapped by contractions but with the cervix closed.
The works of Edgar Allan Poe drown in BPM II.

BPM III = cosmic struggle through the birth canal.
Most movies and TV shows center here.

BPM IV = emergence, birth, and rebirth.
This level is so rich in cosmically powerful emotions and symbolic expressions that it has produced a whole arm of perinatal Grofian psychocriticism, as discussed on page 64.

USING GROF'S MAP TO UNDERSTAND MOVIES

The movie *Pink Floyd: The Wall* provides a rich source to demonstrate **four-level Grofian psychocriticism**[18] and more notably represents a typical psycholytic experience because it visits all four levels rather than experiencing one grand ego-transcendent state of transpersonal. The movie presents a day in the life of a bum-tripping musician, Floyd "Pink" Pinkerton, who ricochets among his mind's four Grofian levels. As the camera zooms in to his eye, the opening lyrics alert us, "If you wanna find out **what's behind these cold eyes** / You'll have to claw your way through this / Disguise."[19] With figure 5.1 on page 60 serving as a map, we are embarking on a psychological four-level adventure into Pink's mind.

In the first level, abstract and aesthetic, reality is presented as a trashed hotel room and later as a garishly violent concert. From time to time Pink's emotions link to the autobiographical or psychodynamic level of personal memories, done in a visual photographic style, reminiscent of old photographs and home movies. In powerful animation we see Pink sinking still lower to his perinatal level. "Behind these cold eyes" the images and memories take on perinatal intensity, nightmarish cosmic flavors, and mythopoetic themes as powerful archetypical images dominate, expressed with extraordinary animation.

In a BPM III "trial scene" of the movie's last few minutes, psychologically extreme animation adrenalizes its viewers, symbolically elaborates earlier themes, and mixes them with magnified psychedelicized imagery: intensified sounds, visuals, emotions, and symbols—"on acid," as the expression goes. In a cataclysmic, cathartic, and transpersonal finale, Pink breaks down his psychological barrier by knocking down the wall of cold, emotional separateness that led him to live a meaningless life as one brick in society's many walls.

The movie ends with a serene BPM IV scene. With light, uplifting music, we see young children cleaning up after what looks like a combination of the rubble from a WWII bombing and perhaps debris from a post-concert riot.

An important point in Grof's theory is that these levels constantly evoke each other by following emotional themes and imagery in an overall composition similar to four staffs in vocal music. At any time, one level may be most dominant, but the others are active too and ready to emerge. The "we're-all-bricks-in-the-wall" scene portrays this: an autobiographical memory of a punishing schoolmaster morphs into an assembly line of children with BPM II–flavored intensity, which in turn morphs into a social meat grinder of archetypical symbolic intensity.

Movies, novels, and TV shows frequently yet unintentionally express Grof's wider four-level theory, often dwelling on scenes that activate perinatal feelings, notably the struggles of BPM III. I've used Grof's general theory to shed light on ***Brainstorm***[20] and ***Snow White.***[21] Kackar and I analyzed ***Fight Club;***[22] as its title and violence suggest, a very BPM III movie.

GROF'S PERINATAL INTERPRETATIONS

Grof himself has made powerful use of his model.

History and the Rhetoric of War
In "The Perinatal Roots of War, Revolutions, and Totalitarianism," Grof demonstrated that **political and military leaders use perinatal imagery**[23] to whip up their people into warlike moods. From Alexander the Great to Hitler, perinatal imagery has reached deep into people's minds by stirring up unconscious memories of their perinatal experiences. In **Hitler,**[24] we see the BPM I of an imaginary past golden age of the Germanic peoples. Losing World War I, colonies, and land, accompanied by the economic disaster of the depression, activated BPM II feelings of constriction and its concomitant desire for more room (*Lebensraum*);

and, of course, the way out of BPM II is the fighting, struggle, and war of BPM III leading to the birth of the BPM IV of the glorious thousand-year Reich.

Art Criticism

Grof points to Swiss painter **H. R. Giger as a master of BPM II;**[25] his work typically shows powerful machines crushing babies and similar grotesque situations. In his book *LSD Psychotherapy,* Grof presented numerous illustrations by himself and his patients. He is a talented artist; early in his life, he planned to become a film cartoonist—one of the few ways to make political comments in Czechoslovakia in those days. In another book, *Beyond Death,* he and his wife, Christina, collected **images of dying and transcendence cross culturally;**[26] they largely depict BPMs III and IV. This led to their being chosen as special effects consultants for the death-rebirth scene in the movie *Brainstorm.*

Cross-disciplinary Studies

With the humanities and psychedelic theory sharing their interest in the nature of the human mind, we might expect findings in one discipline to have implications in others. Psychedelics uncover perinatal springs that flow into multiple streams of social life. In the following quotation from Grof, we see psychology, philosophy, religion, politics, and science come together,

> independent of the individual's cultural and religious background. In my experience, everyone who has reached these [perinatal] levels develops convincing insights into the utmost relevance of the spiritual dimensions in the universal scheme of things. Even hard-core materialists, **positively oriented scientists and skeptics and cynics, and uncompromising atheists** and intellectual crusaders such as Marxist philosophers suddenly became interested in a spiritual search after they confronted these [perinatal] levels in themselves.[27]

This statement backs the claim that humans can develop spiritual interests from psychedelic experiences, and it offers a source of evidence; however, the idea suffers a chilling effect because current laws forbid the best evidence—psychedelic experience. Likewise, because the scholarly community nonchalantly dismisses psychedelic-derived ideas, it impoverishes the world of ideas. Censorship of ideas runs through the legal-academic-political-social complex.

OTHERS'
PERINATAL INTERPRETATIONS

Other scholars have found perinatal interpretations a fruitful path too. They pop up in unexpected places. I was surprised one Sunday to discover correspondences while singing Martin Luther's hymn "A Mighty Fortress Is Our God," outlined in figure 5.2 on page 68.

Mark B. Ryan, at that time titular professor of international relations and history at the Universidad de las Americas in Puebla, Mexico, spotted **perinatal elements in the Gettysburg Address.**[28] Similarly, one of my students wrote an insightful perinatal interpretation of Churchill's "Iron Curtain" speech. Because the feelings that produce these images come from the deep BPM unconscious, people who use them may do so completely unaware of their origins. They just feel right to the speakers and to their audiences.

Art

In a series that dramatically portrays the BPMs, **sixty-one drawings by Sherana Harriette Frances document the inner psychedelic journey.**[29] Her remarkable drawings range across Grof's four-level theory, including powerful BPM images, and, as during therapy sessions, they do not always appear in numerical birth order.

Grof's BPM I— The Good Womb Safe, secure, no worries, relaxed, all needs taken care of	A mighty fortress is our God, a bulwark never failing;
Transition BPM I to BPM II	our helper he, amid the flood of mortal ills prevailing.
BPM II—Contractions Trapped in agony, helplessness, hopeless, meaningless	For still our ancient foe does seek to work us woe; his craft and power are great, and armed with cruel hate, on earth is not his equal.
BPM III—Through the Birth Canal, Cosmic Struggle Fighting against terrible odds. Seeming to die but being rescued "from without" by magic, an amulet, or phrase, or by a supernatural force. Apparent death turns into rebirth. Leaving an old life for a better new one.	Did we in our own strength confide, our striving would be losing, were not the right Man on our side, the Man of God's own choosing. You ask who that may be? Christ Jesus, it is he; Lord Sabaoth his name, from age to age the same; and he must win the battle. And though this world, with devils filled, should threaten to undo us, we will not fear, for God has willed his truth to triumph through us. The prince of darkness grim, we tremble not for him; his rage we can endure, for lo! his doom is sure; one little word shall fell him. That Word above all earthly powers no thanks to them abideth; the Spirit and the gifts are ours through him who with us sideth. Let goods and kindred go, this mortal life also; the body they may kill:
BPM IV—Birth	God's truth abideth still; his kingdom is forever!

Fig. 5.2. Perinatal Analysis of Luther's "A Mighty Fortress Is Our God"

Philosophy

In "Sartre's Rite of Passage," Thomas Riedlinger analyzed **Sartre's mescaline experience**[30] as unresolved BPM II, which flavored his philosophy thereafter. A "cardboard world" of meaningless suffering, a sense of being trapped, a "no-exit hell"—these express BPM II emotions and ideas.

Locating Grof's work in a wider philosophical context, in *The Passion of the Western Mind,* Tarnas wrote, "While this perinatal area constituted the critical threshold for the therapeutic transformation, it also proved to be the **pivotal area for major philosophical and intellectual issues.**"[31]

A Menu of Delicious Ideas

University students can easily learn Grofian criticism too. In my *Psychedelic Studies* class, I would present my Grofian interpretation of *Snow White,* then have the students use four-level, or perinatal, ideas to interpret something on their own. Although they usually chose a movie or TV show, their life experiences, such as moving into an apartment or social relationships, provided other examples. In spite of my initial skepticism, one student used her example of buying a new pair of ill-fitting shoes to attend an important dance, all with BPM-appropriate physical feelings and emotions. This assignment turned out to be an excellent way to teach Grof's cartography. Some years I have asked them to interpret Edna St. Vincent Millay's "Renascence." During election years, it's fun to spot perinatal imagery, thoughts, and feelings in political rhetoric. Ads are rich too.

As you travel your life, you'll find that these levels influence your life and the world around you. Grof's theory of rich ideas can help you understand TV shows, movies, and other works of art; can promote your own insights into your emotional life (What happens when you trip off one of your own COEXs?); and can provide wider perspectives on politics and other wide-scale events.

Grofian psychocriticism is off to a good start, but as the next chapter shows, psychedelics and other mindapps are informing the wider intellectual world in multiple other ways too.

How do we move these ideas into action?

Association for Bridging the Humanities and the Sciences

Thematic Conference:
Psychedelic Mind-sources for the Mind-arts—
Grofian Perspectives

6
Save the Humanities!
Psychedelics to the Rescue!

*Many who before regarded legislation on the subject [read:
exploration of mindapps] as chimerical, will now fancy that
it is only dangerous, or perhaps not more than difficult.
And so in time it will become to be looked on as among the
things possible, then among the things probable;—and so at
last it will be ranged in the list of those few measures which
the country requires as being absolutely needed. That is the
way in which public opinion is made.*

ANTHONY TROLLOPE, *PHINEAS FINN*

In June 2013, the American Academy of Arts and Sciences (AAAS)
issued a **report that bemoaned the sorry state of the humanities.**[1]
While the humanities had previously occupied the peak of academic
status, fewer students were majoring in these subjects, financial support
was waning, departments were shrinking, and the humanities were
not getting the scholarly respect that AAAS members thought they
deserved. Pity the poor humanities! Take heart. Rescue is on the way!

As each psychology develops, its ideas enrich the humanities with new understandings of the human mind and new types of psychocriticism. With the **"Psychedelic Renaissance"**[2] occurring in medicine and the neurosciences becoming **recognized in general periodicals and online,**[3] it's time for psychedelic mindapps to make their contributions to the humanities' disciplines. To pull the AAAS out of its situation, doses of psychedelic ideas and attention to other mindapps would advance such disciplines into the twenty-first century with fruitful mindbody-derived ideas. As you read this chapter's scrapbook of brief leads for the humanities, I hope you'll feel that they're clues worth following.

THE PSYCHEDELIC AESTHETIC

A friend of mine who is a retired professor of art history and I have been poking at the question "What makes a work of art psychedelic?" We're including all the arts, not just visual ones. Our tentative answers include intensifying colors, amplifying sounds, distorting shapes, bending sounds, collaging ideas, changing the visual and auditory perceptions of time and space, and so forth. Lists of so-called psychedelic music and art such as those below and found in books approach the topic by listing common examples, but they don't answer the persistent problem by identifying common traits across the arts. "Psychedelic?" They just don't catch it. Just as we hear people describing unusually powerful events as "on steroids," people also say "on acid" to describe all sorts of things. What do they mean? What is the common element or elements?

Art
When you think of psychedelics and art, probably what pops into your mind most often is psychedelic posters. Numerous books and a few **museum exhibitions**[4] have featured 1960s poster art and psychedelic artists in this limited genre: among others the San Diego Museum of

Art and the San Francisco Museum of Modern Art in 1987 mounted displays of poster art. Now, however, the word *psychedelic* is being applied to a general influence on art. In *Psychedelic: Optical and Visionary Art Since the 1960s,* David Rubin, Robert Morgan, and Daniel Pinchbeck see the sixties as starting a new artistic sensibility.

> In addition to possessing abstract properties of extreme color and kaleidoscopic space, a **psychedelic aesthetic sensibility** may also be expressed in the form of representational imagery that is highly imaginative or visionary, the type of art that is often labeled by such monikers as "surrealist" or "magic realist." Within this genre, the terminology emphasizes the imagery itself more than the style in which it is depicted.[5]

Music

Psychedelic music is generally seen as a sub-genre of rock from the 1960s, but an article on the BBC website defines it in a wider sense: "**spacey sounds, a trippy feel, sometimes including Eastern influences and instruments**—then there's plenty from previous decades, and centuries, that fits the bill."[6]

> Debussy—*Voiles*
> Berlioz—*Symphonie fantastique*
> Holst—*The Planets* ("VII. Neptune, the Mystic")
> Ligeti—*Lux Aeterna*
> Scriabin—*Poem of Ecstasy*
> Steve Reich—*Drumming*

And, as any psychedelicist knows, ordinary sounds and mundane daily sights can—under the right conditions—be psychedelic too. Sometimes a wham-bang, at other times a light etherealism. Opposites can both be psychedelic. A spice rack is as psychedelic as a symphony. With a proper dose, any touch, taste, sound, fragrance, and sight can become psychedelic, and so can our ideas and emotions—our inner life can be psychedelic too.

So being psychedelic does not depend on the external objects we perceive. From within a psychedelic mindstate, the overall structure of a symphony might be marvelous; so might one's own thumbnail. It is the mind's intensified aesthetic power that does it, not the object. "What makes something psychedelic?" The common element? The psychedelic aesthetic is intensified brain-mind sensibility, a mindbody state or states. Our minds make things psychedelic, not the objects we perceive.

Maybe *aesthetigen* would fit for selected mindstates too. Come to think of it, what we consider psychedelic experiences and what we commonly call aesthetic experiences have a surprising number of subjective qualities in common. Subjectively, both direct our attention to various sensations (sights, sounds, flavors, fragrance, and touch); they temporarily intensify our focus while decreasing our attention to other things; they direct our attention to an appreciation of previously neglected details; they produce an intensified (even overwhelming) sense of beauty; they stretch our sense of time; and, when most powerful, they absorb our attention to such a degree that we temporarily lose track of our selves. Come to think of it again, just as each of these qualities qualify the standard arts as aesthetic experiences, they also qualify psychedelics as aesthetic experiences, as an art form—an aesthetic form that is interoceptive (in-mind) rather than exteroceptive (residing in outer objects). Works of art elicit these qualities from outside our bodies; psychedelics promote them inside. Yes, *aesthetigen* applies to psychedelics.

NUGGETS FOR THE HUMANITIES

Psychedelic clinical research provides prime examples of interdisciplinary nuggets that are often inadvertently buried in psychotherapy articles. For example, in spite of their titles containing *meaning* and *spiritual significance,* two 2006 and 2008 articles from the Johns Hopkins University School of Medicine offer the social sciences and the humanities nuggets for their lines of research. The following selected items are from table 2 in the 2008 article list **research-rich topics**[7] for the social sciences and humanities.

Positive/negative attitudes about life and self
Positive/negative mood changes
Altruistic/positive social effects
Antisocial/negative social effects
Positive behavioral changes
Personal meaningfulness
Spiritual significance
Sense of well-being or life satisfaction

Scholars of the social relations in the social sciences and humanities can pick these up and run with them. Among the eighty-six items on the ***Persisting Effects Questionnaire***[8] that contribute to these scales are usage

You are a more creative person.
You have more inner peace (i.e., centeredness, serenity, calmness).
You are more tolerant toward others.
Your social concern/compassion has increased.

The humanities and social sciences involve **creativity,**[9] inner peace, tolerance, and compassion too. Other hidden nuggets for the humanities reside in the rich language used when people describe their psychedelic experiences and even in science-rich publications such as *The Journal of Psychopharmacology.* Humanists, read them.

LANGUAGE STUDIES

In addition to the usual quantitative reports in medical and neuro-science journals on psilocybin treatment to reduce anxiety in cancer patients, researchers at the Langone Medical School, part of New York University, reported in the *Journal of Humanistic Psychology* the words and phrases the volunteers used in describing their experiences.

> Verbatim transcribed interviews were analyzed by a five-member research team using interpretative phenomenological analysis. General themes found in all or nearly all transcripts included relational embeddedness, emotional range, the role of music as conveyor of experience, meaningful visual phenomena, wisdom lessons, revised life priorities, and a desire to repeat the psilocybin experience.

Students of art, music, language, and philosophy will want to follow up with more in-depth questions. Typical themes from a majority of transcripts also included exalted feelings of joy, bliss, and love; ineffability; alteration to identity; and increased interconnectedness. Less frequent descriptors were synesthesia; expression of powerful emotions; and the sense of surrender, or "letting go."

In the NYU-Langone study, we see psychedelic experiences providing the **language for semiotic analysis.**[10] Professor Neşe Devenot, now at Case Western Reserve School of Medicine, took a different tack. In "Medical Ecstasies: Chemical Synthesis and Self-Experimentation in **Romantic Science and Poetry,**"[11] she "shows how Romantic poetic experiments (by Coleridge and Wordsworth) were designed like psychedelic self-experiments." In a videotape from the 2017 Breaking Convention conference in Greenwich, England, she showed that psychedelics can **transform how we read canonical Romantic poetry.**[12] I experience this in the writers of the early nineteenth century when they used *sublime*. While my reaction may or may not be what they intended, my transcendent psychedelic experiences give me, rightly or wrongly, a feeling for what they meant.

These are rich leads for the humanities and social relations, but can we expect busy neuro researchers to take the time to write for, say, *The Psychology of Religion* or *Political Economy*? Probably not; to be realistic, they have enough to do as it is. Part of the problem is the way institutions and disciplines are organized. In addition, yearly professional evaluations, which many universities require, are likely to evaluate articles within their specialties more highly than articles outside. But the world of ideas is impoverished by lack of interdisciplinary fertilization. Do I have a full solution? No, again. But the foolishness of supposing that all articles in a journal must all follow the same style and format is one little impediment to interdisciplinary intellectual enrichment that's not hard to remove other than "We've always done it this way."

A hint for young scholars: a hidden secret of how to make original contributions to your field is to read what others in your field aren't reading, then import what you find to your home field to show how your home field informs the newly explored one. This will please the big guns in your field even more; it adds importance to their work and discipline. Nothing works all the time, but with psychedelics being such a rich interdisciplinary field, chances are you'll hit on something. Providing insights from the visiting outside discipline may be even more cogent yet annoying to some of your home discipline's defenders.

NEWS MEDIA AS PSYCHEDELIA'S VITAL SIGN

At the 2017 Psychedelic Science meeting in Oakland, California, several of us whose psychedelic memories go back to the sixties and seventies were marveling about how the press's view of psychedelics has switched one hundred eighty degrees this century. Of course, it's one of our favorite topics, as it justifies our work in the succeeding decades, and it's a real pleasure to see meetings now that are populated

not just by a bunch of gray-heads but primarily by the new generation of psychedelic scientists and scholars. We remember the fear-
thrilling biases of news reports of the sixties: the window-pane and
pill decorated cover story of *Life* magazine in March 1966—"***THE
EXPLODING THREAT OF THE MIND DRUG THAT GOT
OUT OF CONTROL LSD.***"[13] All caps and bold, of course. Lower on
the cover below the window panes: "TURMOIL IN A CAPSULE.
One dose of LSD is enough to set off a mental riot of vivid colors and
insights—or of terror and convulsions." It must have been fun writing
such stories and headlines; a writer could cut loose with a full range of
emotionally packed words and sentences.

If there were a prize for extreme anti-psychedelic rhetoric, I'd nomi-
nate *The Saturday Evening Post*'s August 12, 1967, issue.

> Cover: "The Newly Discovered Dangers of LSD: To the Mind To
> the Body To the Unborn"
> Page 19: **"THE HIDDEN EVILS OF LSD"**[14]
> "New research finds it's causing genetic damage that poses a threat
> of havoc now and appalling abnormalities for generations yet
> unborn."
> Page 20 has my favorite: "The 'orange man' locked himself in his
> room. He said that if anyone touched him he would turn into
> orange juice."

At the very least, the *Post* writers and layout artists deserve
Honorable Mention for packing so many vivid emotionally charged
words into one article. I wonder what it would it feel like getting high
and reading these articles now.

People believed this. "If *Life* and the *Post* say so, it must be true."

If you want to taste the fake news of the sixties yet put it in historical
and social context, I recommend Stephen Siff's book *Acid Hype*.[15] Most
studies of the psychedelic sixties focus on one of several threads: Leary
and his shenanigans, Hofmann and early LSD days, Wasson's search for

soma, politics and activism, drug policy, early therapeutic and neuro-science discoveries, broad social context, or Army, CIA, MK-Ultra, and related matters. The role of the media, if considered at all, was a sort of background music and annoying sideshow. The news and entertainment media, however, wove together these particular threads, and sometimes media grew to become the milieu that overwhelmed society; they controlled public perceptions.

I thought that I had a decent grasp of the complex media story until I read Stephen Siff's *Acid Hype*. It is the study of how public opinion was constructed by the press and includes the usual psychedelic characters as reported in the media, their effects on the media, and the media's effects on them and society. But it fills in links, makes connections, and paints a broad picture that individual psychedelic topics miss, combining Henry Luce, publisher of *Life* and *Time;* Tim Leary; and public scholars. It throws a media-bright light on psychedelic history. At first, TV discussion shows picked up LSD as a promising miracle cure for mental issues, then a discussion topic for mind improvement, then, along with the culture, it played up the dramatic drug-crazed hippies theme. By showing how the media both reflected and amplified the swings in public opinion, *Acid Hype* relates diverse events in a larger than usual pattern as it shows how the media constructed psychedelic reality.

PSYCHEDELIC, ENTHEOGEN, OR *EMPATHOGEN*—WHICH WORD WHEN?

In the light of media distortion, it is important to foster clarity of communication about nontherapeutic topics. In my own thinking and writing, I find it's most precise to think this way:

Psychedelic—mind-manifesting (covers all kinds of mind-manifesting)
   Entheogen—generating spirituality/religion/awe and so on

Empathogen or *entactogen*—generating feelings of warmer social relationships, empathy, or sympathy

Ideagen—generating ideas

Aesthetigen—generating a sense of beauty and/or intensifying aesthetic appreciation, generating aesthetic experiences

See if you can coin another *-gen* word!

Psychedelic means "mind-manifesting"; that is, showing our minds, letting us experience them more clearly and completely. The other five are specific ways our minds manifest, so are subcategories of *psychedelic,* depending on their functions: psychotherapeutic, spiritual/religious, boosting social relations/caring/love, producing new ideas, or intensifying beauty. *Psychedelic* is also the word that dominates most of today's current general periodicals and news stories. From **a list of 104 news reports**[16]—print, radio, and TV—stretching back to 2004 (by far most since 2015), forty-one used *psychedelic* in their titles and/or URLs. *Entheogen* appeared in none.

FRUITFUL STUDIES

In ***The Psychedelic Policy Quagmire,***[17] Harold Ellens and I collected chapters from twenty-five scholars; together they make the point that future policy decisions must consider psychedelics' wide range of scholarly topics and intellectual uses and not limit policy concerns to their medical and psychotherapeutic uses, which dominate current thinking.

In "Chilling Effects 2: Brief Communiqués from the Psychedelic Intellectual Frontier," a section of chapter 1 in *Quagmire,* I listed sixty articles derived from psychedelic research, even leaving aside novels, the neurosciences, and the **vast anthropological literature**[18] on psychedelics. Their disciplines and topics include general social and historical background, mystical experiences, social benefits, mind and psychology, religion and religious studies, culture and history, the arts, business uses and opportunities, psychotherapy, current news, neuroscience and chemistry, and botany. In the 1980s, when I started teaching my course on psychedelics, it was a fringe topic. Except for the *MAPS Bulletin,* there were no new professional or would-be professional articles. This century, the pace has accelerated with, I estimate, new publications coming along each week, and most of them report scientific studies, positive experiences in clinical trials, and reportedly popular uses.

Women's Studies

Including both psychedelic and non-psychedelic reports, **Sisters of the Extreme:** *Women Writing on the Drug Experience*[19] stretches from ancient Greece to the twenty-first century. *Sisters* helps balance the mostly male anthologies with contributions by Charlotte Bronte, Louisa May Alcott, Anais Nin, Maya Angelou, Edith Wharton—some hidden voices and many from within the literary world. Skirting the social persecutions of the times, in 1961 nutritionist Adelle Davis wrote **Exploring Inner Space**[20] under the pseudonym Jane Dunlap, and in 1962 actress Thelma Moss wrote **My Self and I**[21] as Constance Newland.

Ethnic and Racial Studies

A far as I know, this is the field with the smallest number of studies, and therefore the field with the greatest number of opportunities. Nathan Power, a professor of English at SUNY Old Westbury College on Long Island, pointed out that the formerly closed door on psychedelics and **Black experience is now open a crack.**[22] In the movie *The Girls,* the characters drink absinthe, and in *Black Panther,* Prince T'Challa eats a sacred plant. In the talk **"Black Masks, Rainbow Bodies: Race and Psychedelics"**[23] at the 2017 "Horizons: Perspectives on Psychedelics" conference, Power traced the roots of Black America's caution about psychedelics to a history of drug use and family and cultural warnings. Recalling his own psychedelic experiences, he started a bridge of understanding between the Black and psychedelic communities. To my surprise, I learned of the predominantly Black **Detroit Psychedelic Community**[24] and its annual conference.

Although well known for their legal religious use of peyote, Native Americans of the United States are under represented in the wider psychedelic culture and particularly at conferences, while Central and South American groups make a good showing, largely thanks to ayahuasca. Asians are even more under represented.

Classical Studies

Beyond a strictly Grofian approach but providing supporting intellectual background, Ruck, Staples, and Heinrich trace the origins and esoteric meanings of early Greek myths and culture to psychoactive plants, notably mushrooms, in *The Apples of Apollo*.[25] Moreover, classicists may be jollied (or annoyed) to hear that the oracle **Pythia of Delphi**[26] received her inspiration by inhaling psychoactive gases emerging from the earth. Hillman's *The Chemical Muse*[27] identifies drug use as a root of Western civilization.

As ancient history fades into archaeology, readings such as Rudgley's *Essential Substances*[28] and Merlin's "Archaeological Evidence for the Tradition of **Psychoactive Plant Use in the Old World**"[29] include psychedelics yet widen the trail to include other plant-based mindapps too.

Literature—Inestimable Value to the Intellectual

Looking back from the second decade of the twenty-first century, it seems clear that a major landmark in the psychedelic humanities occurred in 1954 when Aldous Huxley published *The Doors of Perception*. Previous to this, Huxley had seen psychoactive drugs only as a way for **totalitarian governments**[30] to control their populations (soma in *Brave New World*). Thanks to mescaline, Huxley's views on psychoactive drugs did a volte-face; in *Doors* he spotted ideas that were to become **future themes in psychedelia's scholarly neighborhood**[31]—direct spiritual experience, Eastern philosophies, intensified artistic appreciation, varieties of perception, recognizing that our minds can function in additional ways, especially "**Mind at Large**—this is an experience of inestimable value to everyone and especially to the intellectual."[32] *Doors* reported his insights that a psychoactive drug could add experimental depth to what had previously been only ideas. My psychedelic colleagues and I report similar results.

In his last book, the novel *Island,* he described an imaginary drug, moksha—"Give us this day our daily faith, but **deliver us, dear God, from beliefs.**"[33] Huxley's psychedelic colleague and friend Huston Smith reported, ". . . nothing was more curious, and to his way of thinking, more important than the role that **mind-altering plants and chemicals have played in human history.**"[34] Do today's humanists have the intellectual courage to replicate Huxley's adventure in ideas?

As a literary novelist and essayist, Huxley's publication primarily reached literary readers but few in the general population. The **spark that ignited the psychedelic culture**[35] happened three years later (1957) when *Life* magazine (circulation 5.7 million) published the cover story "Seeking the Magic Mushroom" by R. Gordon Wasson. "Hundreds of beat and hippie mushroom seekers (including some **leading rock stars,**[36] such as Mick Jagger, John Lennon, and Peter Townshend) made pilgrimages to Maria Sabina's remote Oaxacan village." Perhaps not to be outdone by *Life,* the next year *The Saturday Evening Post* (circulation 5.2 million) published Huxley's **"Drugs that Shape Men's Minds."**[37]

Ethnobotany—The Psychedelic Poet Meets the Psychedelic Banker

Mycologist R. Gordon Wasson and his wife, Valentina—he a vice president of J. P. Morgan & Co. and she a pediatrician from Russia—became interested in why he was a *mycophobe* and she a *mycophile,* as they coined it. One thing led to another and another and another as they explored why some cultures worldwide honored mushrooms and others detested them, particularly psychoactive ones. Brown lists ninety-seven **Wasson publications,**[38] mostly by Gordon, as Valentina died in 1986. Just as Huxley spotted humanistic implications of psychedelics, the Wassons recruited anthropology, biology, and archaeology. Apparently, they hinted at medicine too.

Poet-essayist Robert Graves also played a pivotal role in the birth of mid-twentieth century psychedelic scholarship via his correspondence with banker-mycologist R. Gordon Wasson. After a correspondence starting in 1949 about the speculation that the death of Emperor Claudius may have been caused by poisonous mushrooms, "In September 1952 the poet Robert Graves sent the Wassons an article that mentioned the discovery in 1938 by Dr. Richard Evans Schultes, of the survival of the use of **intoxicating mushrooms among the Indians in Mexico.**"[39]

Thus began Wasson's connection with Schultes at the Harvard Botanical Museum and the Wassons' several expeditions to Mexico, where he was the first outsider to participate in a sacred mushroom ceremony.

Valentina's article **"I Ate the Sacred Mushrooms"**[40] in *This Week,* a Sunday newspaper supplement, portrayed her experiences in Mexico. In an attached, related commentary on the Wassons' adventures in Mexico and on their books, writers Jahn and June Robbins reported that Valentina thought that psilocybin would prove useful in studying "psychiatric processes." Although cautiously not explicitly attributing additional uses to her, the Robbinses presciently added "alcoholism . . . addiction . . . terminal diseases accompanied by pain . . . [and] mental diseases."

In 1962, Wasson invited Graves to accompany him on an expedition to Mexico, but Graves declined: "I wish I could come with you to Mexico, but can't. I'm indispensable here. I wish I were Wm's age; **I'd make mycoenthnology my trade.**"[41] The following paragraph describes a different experience from Graves.

I think the importance of the hallucinogenetic [*sic*] mushrooms is
in informing people of the full visual and sensory powers of their

imagination, so that they can afterwards use it to better purpose. With me, the experience certainly broke down a barrier which had been raised in my mind since I was about twelve and had had a vision of the same "knowledge of good and evil" which the mushroom gives one. There has been a new dimension (or whatever the word is) to my poems since that date. I feel that *psilocybe* should be given once, with full precautions, at an initiatory rite instead of that dreary episcopal "confirmation" of the Anglican Church.

Four of Graves's books[42] contain essays on the possible uses of mushrooms in ancient Greece and Rome, both psychedelic and poisonous: *Food for Centaurs; Oxford Addresses on Poetry; Difficult Questions, Easy Answers;* and *Between Moon and Moon.*

Anthropology

Largely stimulated by Wasson's work, the **Society for the Study of Consciousness,**[43] a subgroup of the American Anthropology Association, studies the vast range of techniques (mindapps) for altering consciousness, their effects, cultural functions, and so forth. The anthropological and archaeological literature is vast and growing steadily. Samples are Rudgley's *Essential Substances: A Cultural History of Intoxicants in Society*[44] and Merlin's "Archaeological Evidence for the Tradition of **Psychoactive Plant Use in the Old World.**"[45] Studies of peyote are both historical and current. **Ayahuasca,**[46] a two-plant tea from South America, is central to an actively advancing field spanning psychotherapy, spirituality, art, and at least half a dozen other related fields.

TOWARD A FREE MARKETPLACE OF IDEAS

Huston Smith, Aldous Huxley, Joseph Campbell, Robert Graves—these mid-twentieth century intellectual lighthouses had their psychedelic lights extinguished. How? **A War on Intellect**[47] is collateral damage of the War on Drugs. Now though, new lights are beginning to shine. In *The Psychedelic Policy Quagmire,* twenty-five scholars proposed ways society could benefit from psychedelics if they can be used skillfully. These include not only their obvious biochemical insights and psychotherapeutic uses but also fruitful uses in religion and wide-ranging scholarship. It is time for a new generation of innovative humanists to explore psychedelic landscapes of intellectual inquiry.

These examples and others provide evidence that psychedelics are the humanities' once and future muse. Psychedelics intersect with the curricula of almost all academic majors and those of professional schools. In my Psychedelic Studies class in the Honors Program at Northern Illinois University, I had students from across the curricular spectrum, including the humanities, social sciences, arts, health, business, engineering, and those preparing for various professional fields. Students enjoyed learning about Grof's theory, particularly applying its perinatal sequence to themselves and their lives. Psychedelic insights about the nature of the human mind and its fullest development excited them—the absolute transpersonal and humanistic topic.

Current and future courses could insert psychedelic/mindapp units into their curricula. Whole courses such as the Implications of Psychedelics/Mindapps for _____ are clearly possible now, and graduate programs can become more sophisticated someday if they include psychedelic research methods. I received so many requests from people who wanted to make psychedelics part of their graduate education that I placed "Psychedelics: Hints on **Looking for Graduate Programs**"[48] on my website. With more than three thousand hits, it is my academic site's most accessed item, and email inquiries add to that. Experimental humanities are within reach, although their methods and protocols will have to be worked out.

On a larger scale, there are enough possibilities for psychedelic scholarship to form centers for psychedelic studies at universities, even whole departments. Such centers could draw on departments throughout the university, perhaps the intellectual hybridization of sharing joint appointments; although psychedelic specialties are complex enough and promising enough to need fulltime faculty. If and when protocols for safe intellectual exploration are worked out, psychedelic research centers could provide university-wide sessions for faculty and advanced graduate students. In fact, like it or not, students and some colleagues are already practicing the advanced psychedelic higher education.

The point here is not only that psychedelics have generated intriguing ideas that people would like to follow up on but also that current policy, laws, social attitudes, academic fear, intellectual caution, and public vogue combine to produce a chilling effect on these ideas and stifle psychedelic methods of intellectual inquiry. But there is solid reason to liberate psychedelic ideas.

> As a society, Americans are committed to the principle that the **production of knowledge should be uninhibited** and access to it should be universal. This is the democratic ideal. We think that where knowledge is concerned, more is always better. We don't believe that there are things that we would rather not know, or things that only some people should know—just as we don't believe that there are points of view that should not be expressed, or citizens who are too wrongheaded to vote.[49]

Where psychedelics are concerned, the supposedly free and open marketplace of ideas is neither free nor open. But humanists can open it.

RESCUING THE HUMANITIES

When we revisit the 2013 American Academy of Arts and Sciences' statement about the humanities' current slump, Grof's distinctive BPM theme that we saw in the previous chapter reappears. While the humanities used to occupy the peak of academic status (BPM I), now fewer students are majoring in these subjects, financial support is waning, the humanities are not getting the scholarly respect that AAAS members think they deserve, and departments are shrinking (BPM II). To pull the AAAS out of its BPM II trap, adventures in psychedelic cognition (BPM III) would energize the humanities and activate humanistic scholars. Could BPM-III exploration lead to a BPM-IV rebirth for the humanities? Do humanists dare find out?

How might mindapps enrich the humanities?

Thematic journal numbers

Conference sessions:
Can Mindapps Enrich the Humanities?

7
What Is Philosophy's Greatest Opportunity?

Achieving the Philosopher's Mind

> *[The] essence of great experience is penetration into the unknown, the unexperienced. . . . If you like to phrase it so, philosophy is mystical. For mysticism is direct **insight into depths as yet unspoken.** But the purpose of philosophy is to rationalize mysticism: not by explaining it away, but by the introduction of novel verbal characterization, rationally coordinated.*[1]
>
> ALFRED NORTH WHITEHEAD,
> *MODES OF THOUGHT*

"**Philosophy of psychedelics** is the philosophical investigation of the psychedelic experience."[2] That's true, but that's only half the story, the boring half. I propose an additional line of investigation: The philosophy of psychedelics also includes philosophizing with psychedelics. Of course, from a multistate perspective this generalizes to other mindapps too. It is time to move philosophy forward from the analysis of psychedelic experiences to philosophy under the influence/with psychedelics. If philosophy is to become complete, philosophers' minds should become experimental variables.

Most philosophical research about psychedelics so far has had to do with the entheogenic uses of psychedelics and the philosophy of religion, such as that of **Alan Watts**[3] and **Aldous Huxley.**[4] Psychedelic culture primarily follows the same track. **Breaking Convention,**[5] a conference held biannually in England, had a philosophy and mysticism track at its 2017 meeting, mostly about trying to use philosophical concepts to understand psychedelic experiences. As a search for "psychedelic philosophy" online will indicate, most of today's popular philosophy such as what is seen on Facebook pages shows the spiritual-mystical-religious bent too.

I have no complaint with this direction itself. I think it's worthwhile: from 1994 to 2001, I spent most of my professional efforts compiling an **online archive**[6] that lists 550 items—books, topical issues of periodicals, theses, and dissertations (no single articles, too many for my time). It provides extended bibliographic information and textual excerpts mostly in the hundreds of words and occasionally in the thousands. This is all well and good, but it's time to intentionally open an additional experiential line for the philosophy of psychedelics. Or should we say "the psychedelics of philosophy"?

EXPERIENCED LEADERS

The idea that our minds can produce many mindbody states and that useful abilities may reside in them is not new. In 1902, **William James**[7] expressed it in what is probably its best-known iteration.

> Some years ago I myself made some observations on this aspect of nitrous oxide intoxication, and reported them in print. One conclusion was forced upon my mind at that time, and my impression of its truth has ever since remained unshaken. It is that our normal wak-

ing consciousness, rational consciousness as we call it, is but one special type of consciousness, whilst all about it, parted from it by the
filmiest of screens, there lie potential forms of consciousness entirely
different. We may go through life without suspecting their existence;
but apply the requisite stimulus, and at a touch they are there in all
their completeness, definite types of mentality which probably somewhere have their field of application. No account of the universe in
its totality can be final which leaves these other forms of consciousness quite disregarded. How to regard them is the question,—for
they are so discontinuous with ordinary consciousness.

Although this quotation is well known, its first sentence is often
omitted. I suppose that even though James was the first American to
teach a course in psychology many people still think it naughty of him
to have used the psychoactive drug nitrous oxide to generate this insight.
But thanks to psychedelics and other mindapps both naughty and nice,
ways of parting our filmy screens have regained power, reliability, and
credibility. This book applies James's assumption that "definite types of
mentality . . . probably somewhere have their field of application" to the
intellectual world.

Of course, this is not to say that every idea or experience in non-
default states will hold up to singlestate scrutiny or be useful any more
than every idea in our default state is worthwhile. An apocryphal story
about William James illustrates this. During a nitrous oxide session, it is
rumored, he had what seemed to him at the time to be a key insight into
understanding the universe; so he wrote it down. When he returned to
his normal state, he saw that his cosmically profound insight turned out
to be comically profound.

Hogamus, Higamous
Man is polygamous.
Higamous, Hogamus,
Woman is monogamous.[8]

However, James is generally in good psychoactive company. In **"The Psychedelic Influence on Philosophy,"** [9] Peter Sjöstedt-H identified thirteen philosophers, from Plato to the twenty-first century, whose philosophizing was influenced by various psychoactive substances. Some are part of the philosophical canon: Schopenhauer and Nietzsche, for example. Others are generally second-stringers: Humphry Davy, Thomas de Quincey, and Ernst Jünger, among others. Sjöstedt-H's list raises a nice question: Will accepting psychedelics and other mind-apps as methods of philosophical inquiry reframe what it means to be a significant first-string philosopher? Sounds like a hot seminar topic for philosophers' meetups. The works of three other contemporary psychedelic-informed philosophers ignite more discussions in contentious seminars: Jean-Paul Sartre, Michel Foucault, and Huston Smith.

Jean-Paul Sartre

It's clear that **Sartre took mescaline,** [10] but did his one-off bad trip set the tone of his subsequent philosophy, perhaps only intensifying his already sour outlook? As we saw in chapter 5, Riedlinger identified many of Sartre's short-term reactions to the mescaline and his subjective reports as expressing unresolved birth memories that were intensified by events in his daily life and childhood. The combined effects of these, Riedlinger interprets, influenced Sartre's view of the world and philosophy. Here is another symposium topic for psychedelic philosophers: If someone's life experiences influence their philosophy, won't the overwhelming power of psychedelic experiences influence them too? Can we see this in other philosophers?

Michel Foucault

Foucault took LSD in Death Valley, California, in 1975. Pieter Stokkink, whose doctoral thesis was on the role of religion and spirituality in Foucault's works, reported:

> According to the men who accompanied Michel Foucault on his first LSD trip, the **experience was deeply transformative.** [11] The

result was a change in his approach in his research, shelving hundreds of pages of his *History of Sexuality* and effectively starting from scratch. . . . The famous LSD trip took place during the transition between his genealogy and his ethics.

Here is a hint for an experiment that will never be done. Take a group of established philosophers, give half of them a powerful LSD experience and the other half a placebo and compare how many attend to mindapps somewhat or even restart their careers from scratch. A pilot, small sample, even N = 1, proof-of-concept study would not be so hard to do.

Huston Smith

In ***Cleansing the Doors of Perception,***[12] Huston Smith, philosopher of comparative religion, chided:

> I found myself amused, thinking how **duped historians of philosophy** had been in crediting the originators of such worldviews with being speculative geniuses. Had they had experiences such as mine (subsequent chapters of this book suggest that some *had* had such experiences) they need have been no more than hack reporters.[13]

Without specifically daring them, Smith challenges historians of philosophy to replicate his LSD experience.

What I really admire about these philosophers is that Smith, Sartre, and Foucault were not outsiders merely observing others' accounts of psychedelic experiences, but they became part of the action. To what degrees were Sartre's, Foucault's, and Smith's insights informed by their experiences? Will philosophers who have similar experiences gain insight into their own works?

There may be more mindapp philosophers—both psychedelic and others—than we're aware of. Sjöstedt-H's full list in "The Psychedelic Influence on Philosophy" traced **psychedelics' influence through**

the works of thirteen philosophers:[14] Plato, de Quincey, Davy, Schopenhauer, Nietzsche, James, Bergson, Benjamin, Jünger, Paz, Marcuse, Sartre, and Foucault. "Outsight," he writes, referring to Humphry Osmond's idea, "was the greatest thing that never happened to psychedelics." Osmond hoped to collect "personal reflections on the experience of taking mescaline by 50 to 100 notable subjects in philosophy, literature, and science."

Will mindapps—both psychedelic and non-psychedelic—become a fruitful path for philosophers and for others who interpret their writings? The multistate woods are full of mindapp questions.

MENUS OF QUESTIONS FOR MULTISTATE PHILOSOPHERS

Can philosophy, which purports to value knowledge, the human mind, and its functions and possibilities, not pay attention to the burgeoning intellectual psychedelic context, to the advances in psychedelic psychotherapy and neuroscience, to information about the multistate range of the mindbody states, and to the mindapps for reaching them? As a nonphilosopher, I presume to present here some topics, questions, and information that I hope philosophers will address in building multistate philosophy. An assumption: knowledge of mindbody states counts as knowledge, at the very least, knowledge about our minds.

History of Philosophy

As a multistate psychologist, I hope that philosophers will help me understand and answer some questions.

- What do philosophers have to say about multiple mindbody states? Do they obscure them with the singlestate fallacy, or do they recognize the multistate mind as a valuable and significant part of human nature?

- Do they use these states in their own philosophizing? Did historical philosophers? If so, did they access these states intentionally, or was it merely by accident?
- Will multistate philosophers develop skill at moving from one state to another?
- Do they devise ways to transfer ideas "across state lines"? The transfer of memory, such as remembering dreams, deserves attention, both philosophical and psychological.
- Did the Enlightenment philosophers limit legitimate reason to the thinking processes of only our ordinary default mindbody state?
- Whatever philosophical topic one is considering, shouldn't current philosophers ask, "How does this vary from mindbody state to mindbody state?"
- Who has the knowledge to contribute to these topics? That is, who gets to answer these questions, and by what standards is one qualified as well informed?

An exhaustive analysis of all human thinking has to include thinking as it exists in all currently known mindbody states as well as in synthetic mindbody states yet to be invented. How might philosophers experience a wide enough sample of mindbody states to make general, valid statements about human thinking? How many states? Which ones? This is enough to keep several generations of philosophers philosophizing.

Metaphysics
"Empirical Metaphysics"[15] is the lead chapter in philosopher of religion Huston Smith's *Cleansing the Doors of Perception*. LSD helped him visualize an idea he already knew about.

Along with "psychological prism," another phrase occurred to me: empirical metaphysics. Plotinus's emanation theory, and its more detailed Vedantic counterpart, had hitherto been only conceptual theories for me. Now I was *seeing* them, with their descending bands spread out before me.

Would today's philosophers benefit from visualizing their ideas? Do metaphysicians dare test Smith's research method?

In a real sense, multistate philosophy proposes a meta-philosophical view. The idea of residence proposes that one's mindbody state is the origin of one's philosophy; that is, our mindapps and their respective mindbody states provide the meta-philosophical positions (conscious or unconscious) of our ideas and our thinking processes. Thanks to psychedelics, they've become more experimental.

Epistemology

In singlestate philosophy, knowledge comes through sense perception and reason. In multistate philosophy, perception and reason vary from one mindbody state to another. Can this produce apparent knowledge that can't, or doesn't, occur in our ordinary state? For example, during psychotherapy with LSD, **Grof's patients**[16] reported knowing things such as their own birth experiences, ancestral and historical memories, rituals from ancient Egypt, and scientific knowledge that there would have been no usual way for them to know. Does this even qualify as knowledge? While today we can easily discount this as knowledge that people may have picked up at random due to TV, magazines, the internet, and other widespread sources of information, some of Grof's early patients were rural peasants who had little contact with the wider world of knowledge. As Grof points out, the source of this knowledge and its transmission are unknown. Other than simply denying these events, how are singlestate philosophers to think about them? The section "Investigating Impossibilities" in chapter 4 provides other apparent anomalies and promotes mindapps as ways to produce and study them.

Ontology

"This is real. This is really real. This is realer than real!" say many people who experience non-psychedelic or psychedelic mystical experiences. Other than simply dismissing them, how can ontologists approach such statements? The opposite is also a common psychedelic experience. "This world isn't real. It's all a cardboard simulation, a matrix we're caught in." What is it that these psychedelic explorers are reporting? We may stipulate that time, space, and matter are real, but our experiences of time, space, and matter depend on the mindbody state we experience them in.

- Is there an internal, mental sense of what is real?
- Are these mind-based senses a sort of internally generated cognitive qualia? Are there others? Truth? Beauty? Sacredness?
- Can they be "rheostated" up and down?
- Other than the hope that evolution has favored us by chance with the best of all senses of reality, what standards shall we use to judge sense of reality as it changes from mindbody state to mindbody state?
- "What are the factors that facilitate the experience of **foundational reality**?"[17] Ralph W. Hood Jr., as author of the standard instrument for evaluating mystical experiences, *The Mysticism Scale,* and as a professor of psychology at the University of Tennessee at Chattanooga and who is highly regarded in the psychology of religion, is well qualified to raise this topic. He questions are they "genuine encounters and not simply [mental] constructions?"
- If they are simply mental constructions, are some of our default state ideas also mere mental constructs?
- Who has the knowledge and experience to decide these issues? Experimental ontology? During DMT and ayahuasca sessions, people often experience entities that they perceive as being as real as things they perceive in their default mindbody states, but the entities do not fit into our ordinary state's reality.

We have, in effect, conflicting realities. These conflicts are not just conflicting statements or propositions but in fact different felt realities, and they are experimentally open to adventurous ontologists. Biological anthropologist Michael Winkelman proposes that our innate brain-based thinking processes such as our tendency to give human characteristics to things, assume they have intentions, imagine that they cause things to happen, and have other humanlike traits **produce seemingly realistic experiences.**[18] DMT and ayahuasca send our automatic thinking processes (operators) and "innate intelligences" haywire. We are experimentally investigating how these psychological operators and innate intelligences (independently or as a group) vary from mindbody state to mindbody state.

This brings to mind Shanon's insights that **ayahuasca and cognitive psychology**[19] can inform each other. Is this also an opportunity to study how operators and automatic thinking processes vary from mindbody state to mindbody state? Just as he discovered new parameters for cognitive psychology, will psychedelics lead experimental ontologists to reframe ontology? Perhaps they will notice otherwise neglected aspects of reality and how they can change. University philosophy courses could become a lot more insightful, interesting, and fun. Psychedelics and other mindapps take us beyond armchair speculation to experimental studies.

Logic

Contradictory statements[20] may both be felt and accepted as true during mystical experiences. This **paradoxicality,**[21] as it is called, is one of the standard traits of mystical experiences; opposites are often seen as two sides of the same coin. William James called this **"reconciliation."**[22] He said, "It is as if the opposites of the world, whose contradictoriness and conflict make all our difficulties and troubles, were melted into unity." Is logic, as we know it, simply an operation of our default state? In some forms of advanced mathematics, there are parallel lines that meet and N-dimensional space. Do other mindbody states open the door to analogous forms of logic and assumptions?

Ethics and Moral Philosophy

On occasion psychedelics produce a sense of a good that is both profoundly fascinating and powerfully puzzling. It doesn't fit our usual categories of good. It isn't felt as a goodness that is the expression of the values of a community, not a socially conforming goodness. It isn't a rational judgment, "this-will-benefit-all-humanity" type of social-benefit goodness. And it isn't an extreme body-based goodness, not some kind of a super-duper orgasmic kind of goodness. It's another kind of good that seems directly experienced in itself—a sort of pure good—not attached to community standards, humane benefit, bodily pleasure, or other things. A no-context good.

The overwhelming sense that "this is good," even "the ultimate goodness," or "the source of goodness" seems like a Platonic ideal, not derived from anything else. On the other hand, sometimes psychedelic experiences produce a sense of evil, dread, or malevolent force. I wonder what informed, experienced philosophers would make out of their own experiences with these value-laden tones. My guess is that philosophy and psychology would have to reach some sort of common middle ground.

Looking back on their mystical non-psychedelic experiences, men reported that before their mystical experiences their **top five values**[23] had been "wealth, adventure, achievement, pleasure, and being respected." Afterward, they were "spirituality, personal peace, family, God's will, and honesty." For women, "growth" replaced "family," "self-esteem" replaced "independence," "spirituality" replaced "career," "happiness" replaced "fitting in," and "generosity" replaced "attractiveness." The experiences they reported on were non-psychedelic experiences of epiphanies or sudden insights that changed their lives.

Similar shifts from psychedelic mystical experiences are documented as lasting at least fourteen months. Embedded in a Persisting Effects Questionnaire given to people who were volunteers in a study of psilocybin-occasioned mystical experience at Johns Hopkins Medical School, an **altruism**[24] scale compared people who had the active placebo

Ritalan with those who had psilocybin. Psilocybin won hands down. It is important to keep in mind that the effects were due to mystical experiences that the psilocybin produced; they were not a direct drug-pharmacological experience. Without the mystical experience, the effect wasn't there. Most important, these results were from carefully selected, well-prepared volunteers who had two monitors staying with them all day on the day of their sessions, followed by professional integration sessions post-psilocybin. We shouldn't overgeneralize these effects to a wider sample of humanity or to self-administering dropping acid until we do more research.

One learns one's values from one's family and society. During mystical experiences, **values frequently shift away from ego-centered,**[25] self-centered identity and personal gain and toward altruism. Fadiman summarized it the following way: "This population may be less interested in materialism, but more interested in productive and satisfying work." What are we to make of this? I wish I knew. We need philosophers who will consider this problem based on their own experiences. Whether they will be a representative sample of humanity is an open question. In his article, "Psychedelic Moral Enhancement" in the *Royal Institute of Philosophy Supplement,* Brian Earp proposes that philosophers of ethics examine psychedelics as a way "to support the existence of a biochemically assisted means of improving a higher-level, flexible capacity **to modulate one's moral and emotional responses** across a range of settings."[26]

Some of the richest questions for multistate ethicists are:

- What are we to make of the senses of good and evil as powerful direct inner experiences?
- Do they set people's axiological orientations to the world and/or motivate people's actions toward moral or immoral directions?
- How do values, ethics, desires, and motivation vary from mindbody state to mindbody state?
- Do mindapps provide ways to investigate ethics and values experimentally?

- Regarding cognitive enhancers and entheogenic uses, is it immoral to prohibit the fullest development of the human mind as current drug laws do?
- Will psychedelic psychotherapy and psychedelic personal growth benefit people who can afford them economically but not people who can't? Will this stratify society even more?
- How are they to be licensed and regulated?
- To what degree are these personal decisions and to what degree societal ones?
- If one country, or corporation, starts to use cognitive enhancers, will that start an enhancement race with its competitors?
- Who has the right to decide which mindapps are legal and illegal?
- Who has the knowledge to decide these issues?

I would find the thoughts of someone who hadn't experienced this sense of extreme goodness as credible as a eunuch's knowledge of sexual experience.

Philosophy of Medicine

As usual, medical philosophy intersects with moral philosophy and public policy.

- Assuming that current psychotherapeutic claims are solid, how should one approach the morality of current laws and policies that withhold treatments?
- Into what morally ambiguous positions does this put the Drug Enforcement Administration, the Food and Drug Administration, and the National Institutes of Health?
- How **does healing vary from mindbody state to mindbody state?**[27]
- Does this question prod medical researchers to examine the various mindbody states to answer this question?

The next to the last question recognizes that mystical experiences produce intensely powerful positive emotional feelings, and positive feelings boost our immune systems. Stress and ill health form one pair, while positive emotions and wellbeing form another.

Philosophy of Aesthetics

Matters of beauty, art, enjoyment, sensory-emotional values, perception, and matters of taste and sentiment are all changed (usually felt as intensified "beauty beyond belief!") by psychedelic experiences. For many readers, Huxley's *The Doors of Perception* launched these inquiries.

> I took my pill at eleven. An hour and a half later, I was sitting in my study, looking intently at a small glass vase. The vase contained only three flowers—a full-blown Belie of Portugal rose, shell pink with a hint at every petal's base of a hotter, flamier hue; a large magenta and cream-colored carnation; and, pale purple at the end of its broken stalk, the bold heraldic blossom of an iris. Fortuitous and provisional, the little nosegay broke all the rules of traditional good taste. At breakfast that morning I had been struck by the lively dissonance of its colors. But that was no longer the point. I was not looking now at an unusual flower arrangement. I was **seeing what Adam had seen** on the morning of his creation—the miracle, moment by moment, of naked existence.[28]

Could any professor of aesthetics want to prohibit this experience to himself or to his students? Or this? Later, looking at reproductions of artwork in a local drugstore, Huxley realized, "What the rest of us see only under the influence of mescalin, the artist is congenitally equipped to see all the time. . . . For the artist as for the mescalin taker draperies are living hieroglyphs that stand in some peculiarly expressive way for the unfathomable mystery of **pure being**."[29]

A common expression for people who have cleansed their doors of perception is that they "really experienced music for the first time" or "became fascinated with color, shape, and texture." Do psychedelics allow us to see the world as an artist sees it? Do they turn up the dial of aesthetic response? Do they do this by increasing activity in the parts of our brains that perceive? Again, we need experimental aesthetics.

Philosophy of Religion

Should we take seriously religious studies programs, divinity or theological schools, seminaries, religious orders, philosophy of religion courses, or similar educational organizations that refuse to expose their students to entheogenic perspectives? See chapter 8.

Philosophy of Mind

We use our minds in everything we do. What we expect of ourselves, what we expect of others, what it means to be a human, depends largely on what we think it means to have a mind (however we define *mind*). As this book indicates, as we move from singlestate philosophy to multistate philosophy, these ideas change, and their implications flow throughout the world of ideas.

Philosophy of Law

In the philosophy of jurisprudence there are topics in addition to the standard central multistate ones.

- How do justice/equity/fairness/and so on vary from mindbody state to mindbody state?
- Do individuals have a human right (in some places legal right) to determine the contents and processes of their own minds and to select the things that influence them?
- In the United States, is there a **Constitutional right**[30] to select one's own mindapps, and do other countries' Charter of Human Rights have their counterparts?

• Do some ideas suffer a **chilling effect**[31] by prohibiting access to the mindbody states that most support them?

In other words, is there a human a right to select one's mindbody state (with restrictions to harming others, and so on)? Don't freedom of the press, religion, assembly, speech, and similar rights derive from this more fundamental assumption of personal mental freedom? Considering drug laws and these freedoms, there is enough fodder here to feed a generation of jurisprudence scholars.

Philosophy of Language

Our language is constructed from singlestate experience and for use within that mindbody state. It is no surprise that other mindbody states are called "ineffable." One of the problems of talking about, say, mystical experiences, may be due to the small number of people who can share their experiences by talking about them. How, for example, could we communicate about the taste of salt to someone who has never tasted it? How can we communicate about other states to people who have never experienced them?

A MULTISTATE MIND PROJECT

The Multistate Project (formerly called the **Neurosingularity Project**[32]) is the discovery, construction, and development of useful abilities including philosophical thinking in all mindbody states, both natural and synthetic. It posits a time when future human brains (and minds) will surpass ours of today. Advances in biology and medicine and related fields point not only to overcoming maladies but also to going beyond that to designing bigger, better, and more functional brains by inventing and installing mindapps. Rightly, most medical research is motivated by the desire to overcome illness or dysfunction, but beyond curing and treating, new neuroscience discoveries may also lead the way to other more innovative mindapps to augment human capacities. Each of the philosophical topics in this chapter needs to be examined to see what guidance it can give to philosophical multistate mind projects.

I particularly like Peter Sjöstedt-H's insight about what philosophy could be.

In fact, it [psychedelic experience] often transgresses the phenomenal criteria by which analysis can take place. But then such novel phenomena can be taken as an **augmentation of the phenomenal toolkit** rather than as a mere anomaly to treat with philosophic disregard.[33]

To be complete, a love of knowledge must include knowledge that exists behind James's "filmiest of screens." He posits that "how to regard them is the question." Combined, multistate theory's ideas—singlestate fallacy, mindapps, mindbody state, residence, the central multistate question, metaintelligence, and mindappAI—propose ways to address James's question; they offer philosophy its greatest current opportunity: multistate philosophy.

How do we move these ideas into action?

Symposia: Philosophical Investigations of Mind Design

8
The Entheogen Reformation

"What was that? How did that happen?" Several sessions after Lake Tahoe, out of the blue, my sense of portent added a spiritual flavor. Religion caught me off-guard; I was surprised when I became interested in religion. Raised in a Congregational church in Connecticut in the town of Storrs, where UConn is located, I experienced church as a social and cultural community with theology, liturgy, and beliefs as side dishes (a sort of kale of religion), something you had to put up with for the rest. It was part of fitting in. Basically, I was unchurched from college until the early 1970s in another university community, DeKalb, Illinois, where I taught at Northern Illinois University.

Did I go through some sort of rapid conversion to become in one mighty swoop a hallelujah believer in an organized religion? Yes and no. "Yes" for my interest in the mystical path; "no" for a specific institution. One day, while tripping, an overwhelming mystical experience caught me unexpectedly. In spite of half a dozen or so previous LSD sessions, this was far outside my expectations and previous experiences. Some additional sessions led to more interests and questions. "What was that, that sense of awe, blessedness, and sacredness? How and why did it happen: was it a biological-brain thing, some past cultural event emerging, something hidden deep in my mind? Why me?" I wondered. It seemed to be heavy with meaning and import. These were new questions to me, personal ones. Most of all, I could see why some people—not everyone by any means—became religious, at least spiritual, by whatever means.

This was then and still is the most fascinating experience one can have, to me at least. No wonder people worldwide sought these experiences, used all sorts of methods to replicate them, thought about them, tried to understand them, and made up explanations. These questions guided me to take religions seriously. Religion really is about something—not for everyone—an experience one could have, not just a millennia-old accretion of habits, history, beliefs, ideas, and social identification. The mystical paths of religions suddenly made sense, not in what they are but in why people follow them, or rather, why some lucky people follow mystical paths.

At every turn, my path was filled with good luck. In 1992, I wrote my first essay on religion and, to get honest feedback from my friends, I used the pseudonym Yon Yonson. I sent a copy to Sasha (leading neurochemist Alexander Shulgin) for his comments and those of his wife, Ann, a psychotherapist. He put me in touch with someone he had recently met who shared my interest, Bob Jesse. Bob and I talked frequently on the phone and founded the Council on Spiritual Practices. When Bob asked me for ideas about what to do, I gave him a standard professor's answer, "Hold a conference and publish the proceedings."

As we planned what eventually became the conference retreat known as "Psychoactive Sacraments," held February 16–19, 1985, at Vallombrosa Conference Retreat Center in Menlo Park, California, good luck struck again. Ken Smith, president of the Chicago Theological Seminary, gave a guest sermon at my congregational church in DeKalb, Illinois. At lunch afterward, our co-ministers, Bill and Jane Ann Moore, mentioned to him that my interest is the spiritual uses of psychoactive plants. Later, they told me President Smith seemed open to the idea.

Sensing an opening, I arranged to meet President Smith at his office. How does one approach the president of a mainstream seminary to ask him for their support about the religious uses of hallucinogens? After days and nights of planning, as I drove to Chicago I nervously rehearsed my spiel and imagined how I might answer his questions.

In his impressive gothic-style office, I started describing my personal experiences and how we entheogenists were not allowed to practice our main sacrament and could even be jailed for doing so. I thought this would take twenty to thirty minutes, but he understood quickly and said CTS would be willing to cosponsor CSP's conference. Then we enjoyed a lunch together at the University of Chicago Faculty Club.

This turned out to be even luckier than I realized at the time. While Bob Jesse took care of local arrangements, it fell to me to invite participants. Recalling my Icelandic days with Huston Smith, I invited him. Later he told me that he was often invited to meetings about the spiritual uses of psychedelics but had stopped accepting invitations. Because they usually amounted to little more than likeminded people sharing their commiseration, nothing long-lasting resulted from them, but with CTS as a cosponsor, something more substantial could result. With Huston's acceptance to attend, the conference gained stature, and my invitations to most others were warmly received and quickly accepted.

Persisting results of the conference included the anthology *Psychoactive Sacramentals* in 2001, later republished as *Spiritual Growth with Entheogens* in 2012. Rather than containing the usual texts of papers presented at conferences, we asked attendees to take into account their conference experiences and contribute their updated ideas. Also, since then, thanks primarily to Bob Jesse, the CSP has supported the Psilocybin Research Team at Johns Hopkins Medical School's Department of Psychiatry.

Beyond merely having these experiences, asking many so-far unanswered questions, hunting for their answers, and considering others' answers, I've found an unending interdisciplinary intellectual paradise, one that has given me opportunities to contribute to **many of the Psychology, Religion, and Spirituality Series.**[1] To me, the use of entheogens is the most enthralling experience someone can have and the most interesting thing someone can study. Thanks to psychedelics used spiritually—entheogens—personal experience, not words, became the ground of religion to me.

THE ENTHEOGEN REFORMATION— A HISTORICAL PERSPECTIVE

What is an entheogen? *Entheogen* was listed in the *Oxford English Dictionary*'s September 2007 release of new words as "entheogen. *noun.* a chemical substance, typically of plant origin, that is ingested to produce a nonordinary state of consciousness for religious or spiritual purposes." And the *Oxford English Dictionary* (2011) defines it as "psychedelics that are intentionally used spiritually; that is, they generate (*engen*) the experience of god (*theo*) within."

Can current religions benefit from psychedelic entheogens? Yes, but it's a culture-wide, decades-long task. If we recognize that entheogens are part of a process of making sacred experiences, often considered revelatory, available to many people—of democratizing them—we see that we are participating in the democratization of religion, a centuries-long process.

Democratizing Text—About the Year 1500

About 1500, moveable type and the printing press democratized access to religious texts. The Reformation and the Counter-Reformation followed. General literacy and public education became important so that people could read religious texts. Concurrently, the growing importance

of words nourished reason and science. While older religious observances of the prior period continued, new word-centered activities
such as reading texts and interpreting them overlaid and overcame the
older religion-as-rite era. New interpretations resulted; new churches
flourished.

Most important, text became an increasingly powerful foundation of religious ideas and a standard for judging them. Over time the
locus of Western religious activity shifted from rites to reading, from
observances to Bible, from participation to verbalization. In *The Case
for God,* religious writer and former nun Karen Armstrong marks the
change in the following way.

> The success of the reformers was due in large part to the **invention
> of the printing press,** which not only helped to propagate this new
> idea but also changed people's relationship to text. . . . [A]nd this
> would make theology more verbose. . . . Ritual was also downgraded.
> . . . Instead of trying to get beyond language, Protestants would
> be encouraged to focus on the precise, original, and supposedly
> unchanging word of God in print.[2]

We need only look at our current religions to see how accurate she
is. In contrast to religion prior to 1500, many people today tend to
approach religion verbally—through words. Holy books, discussions,
beliefs, sermons, catechisms, creeds, dogmas, doctrines, theology, and
so on—all these are words. This overemphasis on words shows up
today in the way we describe religions—as wordy sets of wordy beliefs.
If we ask someone about his or her religion, we expect to hear about
beliefs, not what rituals that person performs. The older rites certainly
remain important to many people but too often lie obscured beneath
a five-hundred-year blizzard of words. As the fifteenth-century
printing-based reformation did then, today's twenty-first-century
entheogen-based reformation offers to enrich religions too, as outlined in figure 8.1 on page 111.

INNER TRADITIONS
BEAR & COMPANY

Inner Traditions • Bear & Company
P.O. Box 388
Rochester, VT 05767-0388
U.S.A.

PLEASE SEND US THIS CARD TO RECEIVE OUR LATEST CATALOG FREE OF CHARGE.

Book in which this card was found _____

□ Check here to receive our catalog via e-mail.

Name _____

Address _____

City _____ State _____ Zip _____ Country _____

E-mail address _____

□ Company _____

□ Send me wholesale information

Phone _____

Please check area(s) of interest to receive related announcements via e-mail:

□ Health   □ Self-help   □ Science/Nature   □ Shamanism
□ Ancient Mysteries □ New Age/Spirituality □ Visionary Plants □ Martial Arts
□ Spanish Language □ Sexuality/Tantra   □ Family and Youth   □ Religion/Philosophy

Please send a catalog to my friend:

Name _____ Company _____

Address _____ Phone _____

City _____ State _____ Zip _____ Country _____

Order at 1-800-246-8648 • Fax (802) 767-3726

E-mail: customerservice@InnerTraditions.com • Web site: www.InnerTraditions.com

Gutenberg and Entheogenic Reformations

Figurehead		
Icon	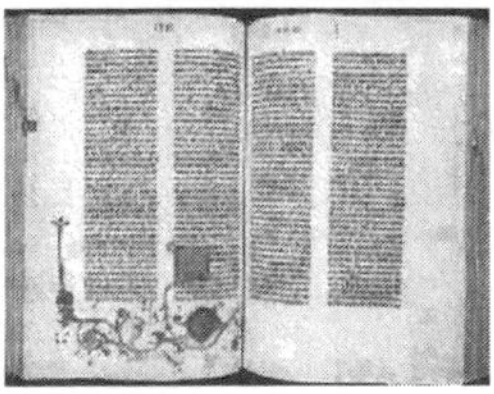	
Democratized	Printed Word	Primary religious experience
Route to spiritual knowledge	Reading, study, thought (cognition)	Mystical experience (unitive conciousness)
Spiritual knowledge	Belief: doctrine, dogma, creed	Unmediated perception
Main academic disciplines	Theology and philosophy	Biology and psychology
Ethical action	Personal: Do and don't do to others	Transpersonal: Beyond self-interests
Education	Everyone should learn to read [the sacred texts]	People need to experience transcendence [everyone?]

Fig. 8.1. Gutenberg and Entheogenic Reformations

Democratizing Primary Spiritual Experience— About the Year 2000

What do entheogens offer religions? First, it's important to realize that in the twenty-first century **a strict process of using them**[3] has been carefully developed. It is not a matter of casually "dropping acid" on a Saturday afternoon. Developed within the medical-psychotherapeutic research complex, current procedures call for extensive screening (not for everyone), hours of preparation with two session monitors, the sessions themselves (one person at a time with carefully selected, largely spiritual music), and follow-up sessions to integrate the experiences into their daily lives.

What do entheogenic sessions provide? This varies from person to person, depending largely on the each person's mind-set, but generally they can provide experiential depth to what had previously been abstract words. To most people who are even moderately experienced with entheogens, ideas such as awe, sacredness, eternity, grace, agape, transcendence, dark night of the soul, born again, heaven and hell, devotion, divinity, blessedness, gratitude, adoration, holy, faith, forgiveness, and others take on new depths of meaning; they become alive.

TRADITION AND INNOVATION
IN EXPERIENTIAL RELIGION

Are entheogenists onto something new, or just rediscovering something old, even ancient? There are enough **books on the religious uses of psychoactive plants and chemicals**[4] to fill a professional library. Their topics stretch back to classical Greece and beyond into archaeological eras. New books and articles sprout monthly and include current neuroscience combined with thoughtful discussions of the brain-mind-spirituality complex. People's interest in experiential religion is both traditional and innovative.

Probably the best-known—and the least followed—example of

progressing from words to experience comes from the ultimate Catholic wordsmith, St. Thomas Aquinas. After building an army of concepts, an **"infused contemplation"**[5] convinced him that everything he had written, thought, and argued "was no better than straw or chaff," and he stopped writing his unfinished book. St. Thomas's preference for primary spiritual experience is widely echoed today, but probably not in a way he would have anticipated. St. Thomas Aquinas was influenced by a non-psychedelic experience of contemplation, a good reminder that various types of contemplative mindapps have the power to enliven religion and spirituality too.

In a very real sense today's lab-based neuroscientists are carrying on Thomas's tradition—although I expect many of them would be shocked to realize it. In addition to promising leads for treating PTSD, addictions, depression, and death anxiety, twenty-first-century research at medical schools finds that with careful screening, insightful attention to the variables of set, setting, and dosage, psychedelic drug administration often facilitates significant spiritual experiences, meaningfulness, altruism, well-being, and similar pro-spiritual effects.

It is mistaken to see entheogens as threatening current religion; they augment today's word-centered religion by grounding it in personal experience. On an institutional level, I hope that theologians and professors of religious studies, philosophy, sociology, and psychology will ask, "How can I update my courses?" It challenges clergy and other leaders of religious organizations to ask themselves, "Can my institution benefit from entheogens?"

On a religious studies level it is worth considering whether an entheogen-based religion qualifies as a **new religious movement.**[6] As defined by Wikipedia, "a new religious movement (NRM), also known as a new religion or an alternative spirituality, is a religious or spiritual group that has modern origins and which occupies a peripheral place within its society's dominant religious culture." Entheology has both ancient and new origins. Chanting, breathing exercises, meditation, and many more mindapps go back centuries, even millennia; the use of psychoactive plants has ancient roots too, but today's psychoactive chemicals look like enough of a break from the recent past to qualify as a new religious movement. Democratizing entheogens away from an elite to the general population marks a huge new step too. Entheogen religion certainly qualifies as occupying a peripheral place, currently.

The description of **quest religion**[7] also fits well: "People with this orientation treat their religion not as a means or an end, but a search for truth." This makes quest religion an intellectual quest, and like any other intellectual quest, it raises more questions than it answers. Divinity schools and seminaries may be places where there is a clear attraction to using entheogens for spiritual quests. On October 17, 2015, Samuel Freedman wrote in the *New York Times* about the "nones," as he called them: "students who are secular or unaffiliated with any religious denomination, commonly known as **'nones,' attending divinity school**."[8] They select these schools not for their theology or for their church-related affiliations but because they offer perspectives on morals and public service. Freedman fails to spot that for some nones (perhaps many), entheogenic experiences are one root of their spirituality and their social concerns.

Another source of entheogen reformers is people who describe themselves as spiritual but not religious. "About a quarter of U.S. adults (27%) now say they think of themselves as **spiritual but not religious,** up 8 percentage points in five years," according to a Pew Research Center survey conducted between April 25 and June 4 of 2017.[9] The same Pew research study found approximately 23 percent of Americans regard themselves as neither religious nor spiritual. Like the nones, from their position, spiritual-but-nots prefer to drop theological baggage and escape weighty ecclesiastical hobbles. Many of them feel that entheogens lighten the load and free the mind.

For some entheogenists, mystical experiences confirm their religious convictions rather than undermine them. For others, they provide escape routes. Entheogens allow people to experience personal transcendent states without linking them to organized spirituality. These varied results show that the entheogenic method is not restricted to any one theological or philosophical position but instead is broadly adaptable to augmenting many positions.

Ayahuasca Takes the Lead

While Americans tend to think of themselves as sending missionaries to South America, in a matter of speaking, we're experiencing a reverse flow now. Two Brazilian-based churches that use ayahuasca as a sacrament have established churches in the United States; like the Native American Church before them, the União de Vegetal and the Santo Daime are protected by the U.S. Supreme Court. Actually, those churches have not so much sent us missionaries as Americans have traveled to Brazil and imported these religions as they returned. In fact, ayahuasca tourism has developed with North American and Europeans traveling to Brazil, sometimes as spiritual pilgrims, sometimes as consciousness curiosity seekers.

On February 21, 2006, the **United States Supreme Court issued a unanimous decision**[10] affirming religious liberty in the case of *Gonzales vs. O Centro Espirita Beneficente União do Vegetal*. The vote was 8–0. Chief Justice Roberts was appointed after the hearings so could not vote. "On March 18, 2009, a U.S. District Court judge, Owen Panner, found that the U.S. Religious Freedom Restoration Act **(RFRA) protects the Santo Daime's use of DMT-containing ayahuasca** as part of their sincere religious practices."[11] This puts the court in the unenviable position of having to decide what is and what isn't a legitimate religion. It's easy to imagine someone claiming religious freedom as a shield for doing drugs, and it isn't at all clear what qualifies a religion as protected by the Religious Freedom Restoration Act and the Constitution.

Unfortunately, when it comes to ayahuasca, the Netherlands has abandoned its centuries-old policy of religious freedom. They shamefully decided that "**infringement of the religious freedom** of the defendant in a democratic society is necessary to protect public health."[12] Appropriate or not, I feel personally betrayed;

four hundred years ago the Dutch gave my ancestors refuge to practice their religion; now they would put some of my fellow entheogenists in jail for practicing theirs.

The religious freedom/law issues are likely to multiply. "Entheogenic Sects and Psychedelic Religions," in a 2002 *MAPS Bulletin,* lists twenty-two psychedelic religious groups and another ten marijuana churches. No doubt some of these have faded away since then, but even more likely, new ones have probably formed (although I suppose many are lying low to escape religious persecution).

Mindapp-Friendly Religions

In the 1960s and 1970s, when psychedelics and other mindapps showed people there was more to life than our default mindbody state and mainstream ways, people explored their own minds, new ideas, and other cultures. "What's going on? What else is there? How can I make sense of this? What does it mean?" In the academic world, philosophy, psychology, the neurosciences, and anthropology picked up young mindapp-knowledge seekers. Popular cultures exploded with many kinds of body-based exercises, breathing techniques, martial arts, personal growth groups, diet-based practices, "energy" practices, pyramid power, crystals, tarot and other "readings," spiritual flower essences, and many more unique approaches.

As people began to have mystical experiences, they looked about for ways to make sense of them. To put it in terms of multistate mind theory, when people started to use psychedelic mindapps to experience mindbody states, especially those that had heightened feelings of sacredness, they started to look for religions that recognized these states, even valued them, and provided alternate ways of achieving them. While the Abrahamic religions have their mystical threads, the connections are usually neglected if not outright ridiculed or persecuted. With sacredness a dominant flavor of some psychedelic sessions, religions that offered a central role for self-transcendence picked up inquirers. This was especially true for Eastern religions that recognized and valued mystical experiences; they attracted psychedelicists, and when these religions offered ways to experience mystical states, inquirers became adherents.

Buddhism is a case in point. Various forms of Buddhism were naturally appealing, and research in the late twentieth century that asked American Buddhists, "What started your interest in Buddhism?" showed that for many Americans, their **psychedelic experiences opened the door to Buddhism.**[13]

What should be the relationship between Buddhism and entheogens? Some Buddhist practitioners believe the warning that intoxicants include psychedelics. Yet many American Buddhists claim that psychedelics provide a glimpse (genuine or fake is contested) of a significant spiritual experience. Some feel that it is best not to get attached to psychedelics and to move away from them. Others think that the two practices enrich and inform each other. I see no reason to suppose that one answer will best fit everyone.

There is evidence that supports this idea of enrich-and-inform. A 1996 **reader and web survey**[14] published in *Tricycle: The Buddhist Review* reported that 83 percent of the responders said that they had taken psychedelics and about half the percentage (40%) said that their interest in psychedelics sparked their interest in Buddhism. Do Buddhism and psychedelics mix? The "nos" came in at 41 percent and the "yeses" at 59 percent. Would they "consider taking psychedelics in a sacred context?" Seventy-one percent said "yes," with the number for people under age twenty rising to 90 percent. A running subhead expressed the gap, "The old were appalled, the young enthralled."

As a particularly fertile field for future mind studies, in chapter 3 we considered, "What might happen if two or more mindapps are combined?" Fortunately there's a study that opens that research direction: **"Psilocybin-Occasioned Mystical-type Experience in Combination with Meditation. . . ."**[15] The high-dose groups, especially if they had mystical experiences and higher rates of meditation/spiritual practices, raised their levels of "interpersonal closeness, gratitude, life meaning/purpose, forgiveness, death transcendence, daily spiritual experiences, religious faith, and coping."

Social Justice

Entheogenic enrichment benefits the sense of religious community, personal values, and social justice too, but these topics are beyond the scope of this chapter. **"Raising Values,"**[16] chapter 3 in my book *The Psychedelic Future of the Mind,* discusses entheogen-enhanced altruism, pro-social shifts in personal values, and related ideas of social service. In the two-volume *Seeking the Sacred with Psychoactive Substances,* thirty-two clergy, scholars, and laypeople propose entheogen-informed ways to **reformulate rituals, ethics, and organizational activities,**[17] past, present, and future. New books entirely or largely about the entheogenic use of psychedelics are being published once a month or more often.

QUESTIONING THE FUTURE

"What would be the impact if the reported positive behavior changes also turned out to be real?" asks Mark Kleiman rhetorically. He is Professor of Public Policy at the NYU's Marron Institute, a highly regarded specialist in drug policy, and author of ***Drug Policies:** What Everyone Needs to Know.*[18] He answers his rhetorical question:

> We might witness, within a few years, **the fulfillment of Moses' prayer:** "Would that all my people were prophets!" People unafraid to die might act differently than the currently accepted norm. Just how much enlightenment can our current social order absorb?[19]

We may be on the road to finding out.

The future is always more about questions than about answers, but in today's questions we may find hints about the future. Four questions and their respective answers raise questions and possibilities about how religion might unfold in an era of experience-based religion, one whose foundation is an intense, personal experience of sacredness.

Belief

How would a direct primary spiritual experience affect someone?

A volunteer in a psilocybin study at the Johns Hopkins Medical School's Behavioral Pharmacology Research Unit answered, "The complete and utter loss of self . . . The sense of unity was awesome. . . . I now truly do believe in **God as an ultimate reality**."[20] Psychotherapist Frances Vaughan, describing her own LSD-based experience, conducted when LSD was legal, says, "I understood why spiritual seekers were instructed to look within. . . . My understanding of mystical teaching, both **Eastern and Western, Hindu, Buddhist, Christian, and Sufi** alike, took a quantum leap."[21]

Spiritual Significance

What if this happened fairly regularly?

Are the changes people feel after an entheogenic mystical experience just a flash-in-the pan, or something more? In both their 2006 and 2008 papers on the effect of psilocybin mystical experiences with carefully selected, mature, healthy adults, the psilocybin research team at the Johns Hopkins School of Medicine reported that, fourteen months after their psilocybin sessions, 67 percent rated it "among the **five most spiritually significant experiences** of their lives" and 17 percent "the single most spiritually significant experience."[22]

As a whole, their experiences also boosted their **altruism, sense of well-being, positive attitudes about life,** and openness.[23] These are results seminaries and divinity schools might envy.

Spiritual Awakening

If this happened regularly, how might wider society change?

Stanislav Grof, summarizing one of the effects of LSD psychotherapy, says, "Even hard-core materialists, positively oriented scientists, skeptics and cynics, and **uncompromising atheists and antireligious crusaders** such as Marxist philosophers suddenly became interested in a spiritual search after they confronted these levels in themselves."[24]

Religious Studies

What if religious studies programs, divinity schools, seminaries, religious orders, and similar religious educational institutions could teach their students to know this?

Professors of religion-related topics—theology, philosophy, psychology, sociology, anthropology, history, neuroscience, and psychology of religion—are a quite accepting group, even enthusiastically so. Classical studies, anthropology, and archaeology have religious interests, and while not specifically oriented toward religion, certainly, the arts, economics, politics, law, and other disciplines and professions intersect with entheogens. I expect that professors who include instructional units on entheogens will find their class enrollments increasing.

Experimental Metaphysics

These changes in beliefs, spiritual awakenings, sacred knowledge, and significance have happened, and in spite of a begrudging society, others like them are happening to thousands of people. They appear to happen rarely in churches or during religious services or retreats. At religious educational institutions they occur only extracurricularly, even stealthily, but in some scientific research laboratories they are occurring regularly, assisted by psychedelics.

Probably the most widely esteemed current reference to entheogens comes from Huston Smith's *Cleansing the Doors of Perception: The Religious Significance of Entheogenic Plants and Chemicals* (2000). Referring to entheogens, he titled his first chapter **"Experimental Metaphysics."**[25] In his preface, Smith refers to Aldous Huxley: "nothing was more curious, and to his way of thinking, more important, than the role that mind-altering plants and chemicals have played in human history." He cites William James's point that "no account of the universe in its totality can be taken as final if it ignores extraordinary experiences of the sort he himself encountered through the use of nitrous oxide." "This entire book," Smith adds, "can be seen as an extended meditation on those two ideas." Smith's position bridges the present and the future.

WHERE DO WE GO FROM HERE?

Just as psychedelics and other mindapps inspire numerous scientific and humanistic ideas, they also inspire myriad spiritual pracrtices and religious ideas. Among them, some trace their roots to historical times, some from current and rich theological writing, and some from fiction.

Devising Something Like the Eleusinian Mysteries

Like the religious past and present, the road ahead is full of promises and cautions. In the later pages of *Cleansing,* referring to the Eleusinian mysteries in ancient Greece where, apparently, a psychedelic sacrament was eaten and/or drunk, Smith wrote, "Is there a need, perhaps an urgent need, **to devise something like the Eleusinian mysteries . . .** to legitimize as the Greeks did, the constructive, life-giving use of entheogenic heaven-and-hell drugs without aggravating our serious drug problem?"[26] And in *Spiritual Growth with Entheogens* he specified, "Find a church or synagogue, presumably small, that is sincerely open to the possibility that God might, under certain circumstances, work through sacred plants and chemicals. . . . A variant on this proposal would be to obtain legal **permission for seminary students** to have at least one entheogen experience in a religious setting if they so wanted."[27]

"What, practically speaking, should be the interface between entheogens and religion?" asked Huston Smith. Respected religious leaders have thought about this problem; they propose that we figure out some ways to augment—not replace—current religion.

Harvey Cox's Moksha

Now retired, Harvard theologian Harvey Cox notes in *The Future of Faith* that many people "who want to distance themselves from the institutional or doctrinal demarcations of conventional religion, now refer to themselves as 'spiritual.'" He sees an emerging Age of the Spirit "in **movements that accent spiritual experience**,"[28] "pay scant attention to creeds," and show "resistance to ecclesiastical fetters."

In *Turning East,* a 1977 book, Cox described his peyote experience many years before.

> What I felt was **an Other moving toward me** with a power of affirmation beyond anything I had ever imagined could exist. I was glad and grateful. No theory that what happened to me was "artificially induced" or psychotic or hallucinatory can erase its mark. "The bright morning stars are rising," as the old hymn puts it, "in my soul."[29]

Perhaps calling on this experience, in *The Future of Faith* he questions, "Might the **capacity for awe be enhanced by a drug** similar to the ones that enhance memory or alertness?"[30] Later Cox mentions a prayer: "Give us this day our daily faith, but **deliver us from beliefs**" from Aldous Huxley's novel *Island* in which daily faith arose from a fictional entheogen, "moksha."[31] Psilocybin, ayahuasca, LSD, mescaline, and similar entheogens are today's real-life mokshas.

WHAT'S THE EVIDENCE?

Looking at the matter coldly, unintoxicated and unentranced, I am willing to prophesy that fifty theobotanists working for fifty years would make current theories concerning the origins of much mythology and theology as out of date as pre-Copernican astronomy. I am

the more willing to prophesy, since I am, alas, so unlikely
to be proved wrong.

"GOD IN THE FLOWERPOT"[32] BY MARY BARNARD

In 2006, forty years after "God in the Flowerpot," Mary Barnard's prophecy is starting to bloom. The article "Psilocybin Can Occasion Mystical-type Experiences Having Substantial and Sustained **Personal Meaning and Spiritual Significance**"[33] appeared, not in a theological journal but in *Psychopharmacology*. From its **extensive favorable media coverage**[34] in the United States, abroad, on TV, and on the internet, it qualifies as a key article, one that opened a trend.

Closer, My God, to Thee?

"**Hopkins Scientists Seek Religious Leaders** to take part in a research study of psilocybin and mystical experience"[35] reads a call for volunteers from the Johns Hopkins Medical Schools' psilocybin research team. Unfortunately, in practice Hopkins limits their announcement for "religious leaders or teachers of congregations and spiritual communities" to what I'd call "pulpit clergy." These are usually appointed by someone higher in their religious organization, such as a bishop, or they are hired by their local congregation. If they offend either one, their jobs are in jeopardy, so investigating the entheogenic use of psychedelics is risky.

Recruiting pulpit clergy is a slow path; professors an expressway. More than that, professors' jobs include exploring new ideas and looking at things from fresh perspectives. They are paid to do this, and new ideas are the currency of the academic realm. Additionally, it would be easy to ascertain any influences that a psilocybin experience might have by observing their syllabuses, publications, lectures, or organizations joined and their activities in them.

Science and Religion

The *and* in this heading is the most important word. Entheogens bridge the gap between science and religion. I found it especially gratifying to see the September 2014 issue of the well-respected journal *Zygon: Journal of Religion and Science*. It contains a four-part section called "The Potential Relevance of Entheogens," all written by authors with established religious credentials.

The title of the article "Entheogens, Mysticism, and Neuroscience" by Ron Cole-Turner, a professor of theology at Pittsburgh Theological Seminary, expresses three intertwined topics from the center of the discussion in which science and religion overlap. "We will discover new ways to think about what happens in the brain when human consciousness is overlapped to richer levels of awareness. What will we make of what we are about to discover?" W. William Barnard, professor of religious studies at Southern Methodist University, examined the Santa Daime church and especially what may be the most fundamental question: "Are entheogens nothing more than hallucinations?" A third topic very much on the minds of the clergy I've talked with is church community. Leonard M. Hummel, a professor of pastoral theology and pastoral care at Gettysburg Seminary cites Huston Smith: "Without a social vessel to hold the wine of revelation, it tends to dribble away." He asks, "Do entheogens produce good fruits?"

The fourth author in the *Zygon* section on entheogens is William Richards. In addition to graduate degrees from Andover-Newton Theological Seminary, Yale Divinity School, and Catholic University, he has a decades-long professional history of practicing psychedelic psychotherapy, first at the Maryland Psychiatric Research Center. Now he combines these backgrounds as a principal session monitor in the current Johns Hopkins Department of Psychiatry's Behavioral Pharmacology Research Unit, which is doing legal psilocybin research. He is coauthor of most of their psilocybin articles and has summarized his decades of thought on this topic in his 2015 book, *Sacred Knowledge: Psychedelics and Religious Experiences*.

Looking at the pillars of religion—scripture, theology, institutional traditions, social concerns, non-entheogenic experiences—in *Sacred Knowledge,* Richards writes, "Primary religious experiences may well provide **wisdom and vitality that may illumine** and strengthen these other religious pillars; however, in my judgment, they do not render them less important."[36]

Later, in the section "Underdeveloped Areas of Religious Thought," he lists some examples of deeper understandings to which entheogenic experiences contribute.

- Theological scholarship—acknowledgment of both unitive consciousness and devotion to the divine in personal manifestations, Christ, Shiva, and others
- Death of the ego—dying to the self and becoming a new being in Christ
- Sin—redemption or salvation as establishing a conscious connection with the sacred dimensions of consciousness
- Religious symbols—a metamorphosis from symbols as intellectual concepts to spiritual realities bursting with significance such as the Eucharist and sacredness of the altar
- Prophets and prophecy—appreciation for the visionary realms that prophets encountered
- Scriptures—written by humans who personally experienced alternative states of awareness

Where do we go from here? Because the entheogenic path of spiritual growth is currently illegal for most citizens, with few exceptions, practice will have to wait, but becoming informed via reading is widely available. Eventually, "perhaps the next step," as Richards hopes, "would be to **extend legal authorization to retreat and research centers,** staffed by professionals with both medical and religious training, who understand the art of wisely administering these substances to those who wish to receive them."[37]

A Sacrament Lost

Children of a future age,
Reading this indignant page,
Know that in a former time
A path to God was thought a crime.

INSPIRED BY "A LITTLE GIRL LOST,"
BY WILLIAM BLAKE

Multistate Theory as a Vital Paradigm for the Future

Multistate theory identifies areas ripe for systematic scholarly and scientific investigation and provides numerous ways to do so. Supported by psychedelic evidence, it meets seven of the eight **requirements for a new paradigm.**[1]

1. *A new paradigm includes previously excluded phenomena.* Multistate theory includes observations about other mindbody states and their respective characteristics.

2. *A new paradigm posits new relationships both within observations and within theory and between observations and theory.* Multistate theory hypothesizes: (1) the abilities of our usual awake state have analogs in other states; (2) additional abilities and cognitive processes exist in other states; and (3) relationships among neurocorrelates, subjective experiences, and behaviors will vary from mindbody state to mindbody state.

3. *A new paradigm introduces useful concepts.* After getting rid of some of the ambiguity of the word *consciousness,* multistate theory introduces the concepts of singlestate fallacy, mindbody

state, mindapps, residence, metaintelligence, mindappAI, and ideagen.

4. *A new paradigm accepts and helps explain anomalies.* Multistate theory helps explain ego transcendence and provides a strategy to investigate other-state phenomena, including so-called impossible events. Some odd events may appear to be anomalies or rare simply because they reside in other mindbody states.

5. *A new paradigm stimulates new research questions and agendas (new normal science).* Multistate theory questions: (1) "How do/does ____ vary from mindbody state to mindbody state?" about all current topics in philosophy, the cognitive sciences, social sciences, humanities, and practically all other academic fields. (2) "How will mindapps inform our knowledge about the human mind and brain?" (3) "How should the next generation of researchers be prepared?" (4) "What policy decisions need to be made at various levels of policy?" To be complete these studies should promote the full characterization, exploration, and development of all currently known mindbody states plus the construction of new ones.

6. *A new paradigm provides new variables, treatments, and methodologies.* Multistate theory presents mindapps as research treatments and mindbody states as both independent and dependent variables. It proposes that scholars use mindapps to invent new forms of experimental disciplines. Multistate theory promotes the construction of new mindbody states and their exploration, refinement, and development.

7. *A new paradigm strengthens professional preparation.* Multistate theory: (1) proposes to extend the professional preparation of humanists, scientists, artists, and other scholars to include the full range of mental processes; (2) proposes that graduate programs provide ways for young scholars to experience these states themselves; (3) by implication proposes founding disciplinary specialties such as the multistate philosophies of religion, sci-

ence, law, and so on; and (4) proposes that specialized professional organizations, publications, and institutes be founded to screen, prepare, guide, and integrate multistate experiences and scholarship.

8. *To qualify as a paradigm, Kuhn says, a paradigm must include a group of professionals who intentionally use this paradigm.* Multistate theory does not meet this criterion yet. However, although not explicitly using multistate theory, the work of researchers cited in this book and elsewhere—their interests, assumptions, concepts, models, independent and dependent variables, instruments, observations, and findings—fit snugly within the multistate theory.

Considering the impacts of psychedelic and other mindapp ideas, in the arts, sciences, humanities, professions, and popular culture, on what it means to have a mind and develop it, there's no argument about the breadth of mindapp influences.

But, is multistate theory advancing toward meeting the eighth criterion, professionals who intentionally use a multistate paradigm?

Though not explicitly using the multistate theory, the works of authors cited in this book illustrate a number of multistate perspectives.

- qualitative and/or quantitative,
- empirical and/or theoretical,
- independent and/or dependent variables,
- observational and/or intuitive,
- recreational and/or clinical,
- sacred and/or secular,
- subjective and/or objective,
- professional and/or amateur,
- intellectual and/or emotional,
- formal and/or informal,
- neuroscientific and/or social,

- scientific and/or humanistic,
- legal and/or illegal.

Recognize it or not, like it or not, mindapps—both psychedelic and non-psychedelic—are informing many of our students, our colleagues, and ourselves. Mindapp seedlings are already sprouting along academic highways. Huxley was right, "This is an experience of inestimable value to everyone and **especially to the intellectual.**"[2]

Syllabus for a Psychedelic Class

This syllabus is from 2013, the last time the author taught this course. URL links have been maintained to preserve this document's historical accuracy. However, at the time of publication some have changed or have been discontinued. We have made every effort to include "(site discontinued)" to notify you if the site no longer exists. Additions or amplifications to the syllabus are presented in brackets.

Go ahead, submit a new course proposal. The worst that can happen is that a committee says, "No." If you're reading a book about psychedelics, you've probably overcome worse emotional crises. Or, you might want to insert an instructional unit into an existing course. I prefer a whole psychedelics course, of course.

The syllabus below is for an undergraduate, interdisciplinary honors seminar. There's hardly an academic discipline that doesn't intersect with psychedelic content, so the content of each psychedelic course will vary so much that each department could have its own unique course, and I encourage you to design your own. Departments that don't include psychedelic content could still benefit from creative problem-solving such as the kind Jim Fadiman describes in **The Psychedelic Explorer's Guide.**[1]

Here is some craft-knowledge I've picked up; some I've tried and some not. Whether it'll work for you, I can't say. But I hope so.

CURRICULUM COMMITTEES

With the explosion of solid research at leading medical schools, there's no lack of top-rate professional articles to cite. As I've pointed out, many of them have leads for topics other than the neurosciences and psychotherapy, so you can select discipline-appropriate background papers. If you are starting by proposing a one-shot special topic course such as "directed research in," "selected readings in," "new directions in," "workshop in," or "topical seminar in"—you know the kind I mean—it may be handy to present your course only as an exploratory investigation, not as having settled, well-known, and accepted content.

Professors like good questions, so try proposing your course with a frame such as "What insights does (your discipline) offer for understanding psychedelics?" Or "What insights does (your discipline) offer for understanding psychedelic behavior?" if you're in a social science. Or, "Does English literature (or Romanticism) shed light on psychedelics?" You'll notice that I phrased these in terms of how your discipline might be used in new ways. Being friendly to your discipline by proposing another use for it is likely to appeal to colleagues who strongly identify with their disciplines. Conversely, "What insights, if any, do psychedelics provide for (your discipline)?" while often more interesting, can be misinterpreted as a threat by insecure colleagues. Better yet, go for both.

With general periodicals and newspapers presenting positive articles about psychedelics, and media and the internet reporting advances in psychotherapy, pointing out favorable press will help dispel academic angst and add "timeliness."

A pitch about attracting new students to your department's courses is a good angle too.

One of the short videos at the **Heffter website**[2] could strengthen your case and at the same time illustrate some of your class material, but I don't know of a curriculum committee that would want to take the time to watch even a seven-minute gem; however, in a covering letter you might give the URL for one or two. If I were still teaching psychedelic studies, I'd definitely have the class watch one or more either in-class or as homework; they are informative, powerful, and emotional.

You should know whether you want to include marijuana as a psychedelic. I don't, but that's a personal call. I see a gap between marijuana and psychedelics, but stronger new strains are narrowing that gap.

ADMINISTRATORS AND THE PUBLIC

Your encounters with administration might surprise you. Without exactly coming out of the psychedelic closet, a departmental chair or dean might say something like, "I was a student in the sixties," or "I've seen some positive articles." The flow of recent news stories is on your side too. If you decide to hand someone something to read, make it only one item and a short one. A stack of articles gets put aside "to read later."

Some of what administrators are doing is **CYA,**[3] so giving them background material from respected sources helps them feel secure about imagined possible challenges. However, I suppose challenges are decreasing as the general public learns about psychedelic psychotherapy.

If someone is worried that you "advocate damaging young, impressionable drug-crazed minds" of students or some such thing, it might help to ask that person to speak to your class about the dangers. I haven't needed this, but I suppose it's a move worth keeping in mind and may make you (or administrators) feel more secure.

If you do run into someone who questions the appropriateness of your course, don't mount a high horse of resentment. Remember, the questioner is concerned about the health of college students just as you are. It isn't an attempt to crush novel ideas or make everyone conform. But it is an opportunity for you to teach someone about psychedelics. It's an opportunity to teach, not a challenge to your professional qualifications.

At my university in 1981, to advertise one-shot courses, we had to put up flyers around campus. I visited buildings that I had previously seen only from the outside and hallways I didn't know existed. A day or so later, my assistant department chair asked me to stop by his office. The assistant provost had called him questioning whether psychedelics were "an appropriate topic for a university course." I mounted my mare of high dudgeon. By 1981, two key books had been published: in 1975, Grof's ***Realms of the Human Unconscious***[4] and in 1979 Grinspoon and Bakalar's ***Psychedelic Drugs Reconsidered***.[5] Not everything was Leary, Kesey, and San Francisco hippies. By great good luck, the paperback edition of *Psychedelic Drugs Reconsidered* had just been issued. It contained a forty-page annotated bibliography, which covered basically all the psychedelic research across disciplines done to date. It was a remarkable project, and *Psychedelic Drugs Reconsidered* is still a book I consult and quote. To make the case that there was valid research on psychedelics, I photocopied the annotated bibliography and sent it to the assistant provost with a vehement letter.

In the letter I told him that I thought his job description didn't include the right to censor course content and that, if he persisted, I'd like to discuss it with him at an open meeting of the faculty senate (or some similar body, I don't remember which). It is the policy at Northern Illinois University, as it is at most universities I suppose, that course content is the prerogative of each department. Since the faculty senate is largely composed of representatives from each department, I figured I'd get near unanimous support. Two days later my assistant department chair called me to tell me that the assistant provost had called him to say that he had asked because someone had asked him. I suppose he was just CYAing. He went to another college soon after, then returned later as president. Motto: Don't be nasty if you don't have to be.

IN CLASS

This is where the fun is. Again, your situation is different from what mine was, so consider this just a menu of possible ideas.

Not Privileged Communication

Although I talked about my psychedelic experiences, I warned my students that I wasn't modeling behavior that I expected them to follow, so if they wanted to refer to their own experiences (by the way, I'd estimate that only about 15 percent of a typical class had had their own experiences) they might want to say something like, "Someone told me . . ." or "I've heard . . ." or "A friend says . . ." or "What about . . ." or some such thing. Most of the few times students have used this tactic, their voices used what appeared to me to be fake, satirical quotation tones, and the class responded with exaggerated eye rolls and snickers. But "non-privileged" is important to mention.

"No credit for 'lab' experiences." Expect to hear some mock disappointed "Aws!"

Getting Things Going

In one of the early class meetings, even the first, it's worth asking, "When you told your family and friends that you were going to take a course on psychedelics, what did they say?" Sometimes, I've made this a question that we'd discuss at our second meeting so they could sample family and friends. Generally their samples were, "You mean they let you?" to "Why waste your time? It won't help you get a job."

to "Can I enroll?" To my surprise, when one girl told her mother and father, their response was, "Good. It's about time." I'd like to have met her parents.

Blah Days

Some days, it seems like it's impossible to start a class discussion. No matter how hard you try, the class seems like a sodden mass, especially early in the semester before students get to know and trust each other. If this happened, I would bring up the topic "What did your school drug program teach you about psychedelics?" This never failed to ignite active discussions, often of a can-you-top-this flavor. "My drug-education teacher told me that her nephew was born with webbed feet because his mother smoked marijuana when she was pregnant." Thank you, D.A.R.E. and other drug education programs, for helping me enliven my class.

Guest Speakers?

By all means. At end-of-the-semester class evaluations, the guest speakers always rated high, and I enjoyed them too. Nicholas V. Cozzi, Ph.D., then a graduate student in pharmacology from the University of Wisconsin, now a leading-edge psychedelic researcher, taught basic neuroscience and basic pharmacology. A Native American talked about his culture's uses of peyote. A mental health professional brought students up to date on psychotherapy. The father of one of my students had previously worked for a government law enforcement agency that caught drug and related law breakers. He brought in some sixties and seventies "Wanted" posters and outlined his agency's work.

I guess that's it. Everything else is pretty obvious from the syllabus, which follows. Enjoy your classes. It's a fun topic to teach.

FOUNDATIONS OF PSYCHEDELIC STUDIES

FALL 2013
DEPARTMENT OF LEADERSHIP,
EDUCATIONAL PSYCHOLOGY AND FOUNDATIONS
NORTHERN ILLINOIS UNIVERSITY

There is a central human experience, which alters all other experience . . . not just an experience among others, but rather the very heart of the human experience. It is the center that gives understanding to the whole. Once found, life is altered because the very root of human identity is deepened.

WILSON VAN DUSEN,
LSD AND THE ENLIGHTENMENT OF ZEN

COURSE OBJECTIVES

Psychedelic research may be the field with the greatest gap between the information scholars and scientists have discovered and what the general public knows. This course helps bridge that gap by surveying the history of psychedelics from archaeological times to the present and by examining their implications for psychotherapy and mental health, religion, and various academic disciplines and professional interests. Students may select a topic for individual study such as archaeology, anthropology, history, psychology, sociology, botany, chemistry, religion, philosophy, one of the arts, literature and language, or implications for professional practices such as health, law, education, and similar fields.

Liberal Education Objectives

In addition to these specific objectives, this course will help teach you to think critically (that is, to analyze information, evaluate opinions, and use higher-level cognitive processes), broaden your intellectual horizons (by exposing you to new ideas from across disciplines, through time, and from different cultures and perspectives), and promote self-awareness (especially awareness of how your own mind functions).

Themes

We will be exploring the following themes through this semester.

The Human Mind
Spirituality
Culture
Elders' Perspectives
Beyond Psychotherapy—Implications for the Mind-Studies
Liberal Arts and Sciences and the Humanities

NOTICES, WARNINGS, AND CAUTIONS

Because this course considers some illegal substances it's prudent to consider this "Psychedelic Warning Label."

Psychedelic Warning Label

Not "Privileged" Communication

Unlike private, confidential communication with a lawyer, doctor, or clergy, communications in this class are not legally given a status of "privileged," so if you have something to say about your own psychedelic experiences or those of people you know, you may want to protect the identity of the person you are talking about. As I have spoken openly about my psychedelic experiences, I am likely to talk openly, but this may not be right for you.

Respect the Power of Psychoactive Drugs

From my own experiences and through readings, I have become increasingly respectful of the power of LSD and other psychedelic drugs. Like any powerful thing, they can be destructive or constructive depending on how skillfully they are used. Among other things, they can concentrate your attention on the most vulnerable, most unpleasant parts of your mind. Therefore, psychedelic drugs should be explored only under the guidance of a qualified therapist, one who has extensive psychedelic training.

If you need assistance, most mental health professionals, as they are currently mistrained concerning psychedelics, may be of little help; some could even worsen your state. Furthermore, street dosages are of unknown strength and questionable purity. Until the time you can explore your mind using psychedelic drugs of known strength and purity under qualified guidance, within the law, I urge you to limit yourself to studying the literature and working within professional and other organizations for the resumption of legal, scientific, religious, or academic research.

COURSE REQUIREMENTS

The twice-weekly classes will each include a discussion, focused on the quote given with the date of the class. These quotes typically express the main idea for that class session. In addition, there will be weekly reading and research assignments such as internet field trips.

Weekly Internet Field Trips. Assigned.
These will transport you to some of the many websites that specialize in psychedelics and related topics. From their home pages, explore around the sites and their links for about ten minutes to see what you can find.

Recreational Internet Field Trips. Not assigned.
Fun places to poke around.

In-Class Videos
These are not recreational time-fillers, but should be considered as guest lectures. You should learn from their contents as you would from

readings and lectures. One of the nice things about this topic is that there are many excellent videos.

Required Books

The following books are required texts for this course.

Grof, Stanislav	*LSD: Doorway to the Numinous* (previous title, *Realms of the Human Unconscious*)
Huxley, Aldous	*The Doors of Perception*
Roberts, Thomas	*The Psychedelic Future of the Mind*
Walsh, Roger and Grob, Charles	*Higher Wisdom*

MAPS email newsletter subscription is available at the MAPS website.

Recommended Books

The following books are recommended reading for this course.

Fadiman, James	*The Psychedelic Explorer's Guide*
Grob, Charles	*Hallucinogens: A Reader*
Hayes, Charles	*Tripping*
Hintzen, Annelie	*The Psychopharmacology of LSD*
Roberts, Thomas	*Spiritual Growth with Entheogens*
Sessa, Ben	*The Psychedelic Renaissance*
Smith, Huston	*Cleansing the Doors of Perception*
Stevens, Jay	*Storming Heaven*
Wolfe, Tom	*The Electric Kool-Aid Acid Test*

And hundreds more, maybe thousands of others.

Current Research In-Class Presentation

While we are studying Grof, people always ask, "Is any psychedelic research going on today?" To keep our class up to date on current research, during the classes of Aug. 28–Sept. 18 and Oct. 2–9, you will each briefly summarize (five to seven minutes) a report on current psychedelic research for the class. Sign up to reserve a date and/or topic. Make a one-page handout, which will become part of your portfolio. The most up-to-date places to look for research are www.maps.org/research, www.clinicaltrials.gov, and www.ncbi.nlm.nih.gov/entrez/query (probably the world's best source for medical news).

Self-Selected Book and In-Class Presentation

Writings on psychedelics are so many, new, and varied that it is impossible to cover them all. To give our class a taste of this diversity, you'll each select (with my OK) a book to read on your own for class. It can be fiction or nonfiction, popular or scholarly, scientific or humanistic, pro-psychedelics or anti-psychedelics, secular or sacred, so long as it has psychedelics as an important theme. You'll reserve a date to tell the class about it, during the weeks of Oct. 14–Dec. 2. You will have about twelve minutes to summarize and evaluate the book. Or you might compare two books. If you want and if the book is long, you may work with one partner and both share a presentation. You should provide a one or two page handout for the class, which will become part of your portfolio.

Your book review should include the following topics.

Bibliographic Information
Author, year published, title and subtitle, edition.
Place published and publisher.
Anything special? One of a series? Award winner?
Index? Illustrations? References? Appendices?

What the book is about
and the author's purpose
Hint: Prefaces, forewords, and introductions are helpful here.
Author's credentials and background.
Author's approach to the book's topic, overall position or slant.

**Intended readership(s). Does the author
write to a specific readership(s)?**

Complexity of thought.

Reading difficulty.

Specialized vocabulary.

Judgments

Is relevant information omitted from the book? Errors? Does it consider other perspectives fairly?

Does the book's physical appearance add to the book, especially art books and books whose illustrations are a significant aspect of the book? This may be irrelevant for many books.

What do other reviewers say? To form your own judgments, I suggest reading other reviews after you've read the book.

Is the intended readership well served? Who would and who would not benefit from reading the book?

Connections

Implications for what we are studying in this course.

The Meat of a Review

The author's main point(s) and your:

- Evaluation
- Reflections
- Judgments

Give the reasons why you make these assessments

GRADING

During Finals Week, you will submit a portfolio whose contents are listed in the Finals Week section of this syllabus.

WEEK-BY-WEEK SCHEDULE

Aug. 26

This week will include an overall introduction to the class, as well as a discussion of psychedelic vs. psychoactive and why not to put LSD in your friend's coffee!

Quotes for Discussion

> It is assumed that if, as is often said, one traumatic event can shape a life, one therapeutic event can reshape it.
>
> GRINSPOON AND BAKALAR,
> PSYCHEDELIC DRUGS RECONSIDERED

> A discipline comes of age and a student of that discipline reaches maturity when it becomes possible to recognize, estimate, and allow for the errors of their tools. . . . Yet there is one instrument that every discipline uses without checking its errors. This, of course, is the human psychological apparatus.
>
> LAWRENCE KUBIE

Aug. 28

Assignments

Read: this syllabus. Any questions?

Weekly Internet Field Trip: www.maps.org to sign up for their free Email Newsletter.

View: What insights and ideas, surprises and hopes, curiosities and questions do the three listed videos raise in your mind?

- www.heffter.org/video.htm 7 minutes [Click videos at the top of the Heffter Research Institute page. For assignments like these, I would ask students to choose a video that most interested them.]

- www.youtube.com/watch?v=LKm_mnbN9JY 19 mins [Youtube: "TEDxMidAtlantic-Roland Griffiths-11/5/09" posted by TEDx Talks. 1 hour 19 minutes]
- www.btci.org/bioethics/2013/videos2013/vid6.html 58 minutes (site discontinued)

Assignments Continued

Start reading Huxley's *The Doors of Perception.*

Sept. 2: No class meeting.

Assignments

Finish reading Huxley's *The Doors of Perception*

Recreational Internet Field Trip: Huxley. www.youtube.com /watch?v=mbI4f1WvN9w 5 mins [Youtube: "Aldous Huxley Doors of Perception" posted by hasidichippie]

Sept. 4

Quote for Discussion

> *Stanislav Grof is widely regarded as the world's foremost researcher of psychedelics. . . . He supervised several thousand clinical and research sessions with psychedelics, considerably more than any other researcher. He has therefore perhaps seen a vaster panoply of human experience than anyone else in history.*
>
> R. WALSH AND C. GROB, *HIGHER WISDOM*

Assignments

Class discussion: *The Doors of Perception*

Grof, *LSD: Doorway to the Numinous,* preface pages xvii–xxx, chapter 1

Higher Wisdom, Grof interview chapter, pages 119–44

Sept. 9

Quote for Discussion

> *Fortunately, after a successful psychedelic experience, you never go back to your previous state of consciousness— that's the whole point of taking psychedelics. If you don't integrate the higher levels of consciousness into your daily life, then the trip has been irrelevant. . . . If a psychedelic doesn't result in your becoming a human being who is more human, then psychedelics are meaningless and don't make a difference. I have never known anyone who had a profound transcendental experience who wasn't significantly changed in his or her daily life by that experience.*
>
> GARY FISHER, "TREATING THE UNTREATABLE"
> (FROM *HIGHER WISDOM*)

Assignments

Grof: *LSD: Doorway to the Numinous,* 34–61

Websites on psychoactive plants and chemicals. Rich, deep resources. [To be provided in class.]

Weekly Internet Field Trip: www.stanislavgrof.com [Stanislav Grof website]

Sept. 11

Quote for Discussion

> *Ah, yes. I see what you have done. You have stripped away ME!*
> *This is a touch of death—a preparation for the big one when No Me will be permanent.*
>
> UNNAMED PATIENT TO DR. SIDNEY COHEN

Assignments

Grof: *LSD: Doorway to the Numinous,* chapters 2 and 3, pages 34–61

Recreational Internet Field Trip: www.maps.org/media/videos (site discontinued) [Search videos on MAPS website.] This collection from April 2010, Dec. 2011, and April 2013 conferences include most of the world's leading psychedelic researchers. This is the best internet collection of psychedelic videos.

Sept. 16

Quote for Discussion

> *The greatest impact this acid trip had on me was to entirely alter my view of death. This has affected the way I live. . . . If I had been asked to draw a picture of death I would have drawn a black box; that is all. Now I have tried drawing pictures of death in which I am fusing into the horizon, feeling ecstasy. My sense was, and is, that the strong beam of light from the setting sun on the ocean horizon will pull me into its orange warmth, and I will sink into a "beyond."*
>
> NATALIE ROGERS, *EMERGING WOMAN*

Assignments

Grof: *LSD: Doorway to the Numinous,* chapter 3, pages 61–96

Weekly Internet Field Trip. www.heffter.org [Heffter Research Institute website] A sponsor of much of the best current research, organizer of annual bioethics conference in Madison.

Sept. 18

Quote for Discussion

> *Last Friday, April 16, 1943, I was forced to interrupt my work in the laboratory in the middle of the afternoon and proceed home, being affected by a remarkable restlessness, combined with a slight dizziness. At home I lay down and sank into a not unpleasant intoxicated condition, characterized by an extremely stimulated imagination. In*

a dreamlike state, with eyes closed (I found the daylight to be unpleasantly glaring), I perceived an uninterrupted stream of fantastic pictures, extraordinary shapes with intense, kaleidoscopic play of colors. After some two hours this condition faded away.

ALBERT HOFMANN, *LSD—MY PROBLEM CHILD*

Assignments

Grof: *LSD: Doorway to the Numinous,* chapter 4, perinatal chapter, pages 97–126

Question: Where do we see BPMs I and II in our lives, arts, and history?

Recommended: Disney's movie *Snow White*

In-class lecture: BPM analysis of Disney's *Snow White and the Seven Dwarfs*

Recreational Internet Field Trip: 1 hr. 29 minutes www.maps.org /videos/source/video_grof.html (site discontinued)

Sept. 23

Quote for Discussion

[T]his substance is an unspecific amplifier of mental processes that brings to the surface various elements from the depth of the unconscious. What we see in the LSD experiences and in various situations surrounding them appears to be basically an exteriorization and magnification of the conflicts intrinsic to human nature and civilization. If approached from this point of view, LSD phenomena are extremely interesting material for a deeper understanding of the mind, the nature of man, and human society.

STANISLAV GROF,
REALMS OF THE HUMAN UNCONSCIOUS

Assignments

Weekly Internet Field Trip: http://birthpsychology.com [Birth Psychology website by the Association of Pre- and Perinatal Psychology and Health (APPPAH)]

Grof: *LSD: Doorway to the Numinous,* perinatal chapter continued, pages 127–56

Question: Where do we see BPMs III and IV in our lives, arts, and history?

Tranche 1: Student BPM papers. Sign up for a spot. Show your ability to use Grof's BPMs to analyze something, an event in your life, a movie or TV show, historical event, news stories, your dreams, literature, music, etc. Make a 7–10 minute in-class presentation and include a class handout, which will also become part of your portfolio.

Sept. 25

Quote for Discussion

> *In contradistinction to writings on the psychedelics that are occupied with experiences the mind can have, the concern here is with evidence they afford as to what the mind is . . . judged both by the quantity of data encompassed and by the explanatory power of the hypotheses that make sense of this data, it is the most formidable evidence psychedelics have thus far produced. The evidence to which we refer is that which has emerged through the work of Stanislav Grof. . . . The novelty of Grof's work lies in the precision with which the levels of the mind it brings to view correspond with the levels of selfhood the primordial tradition describes.*
>
> HUSTON SMITH, *FORGOTTEN TRUTH:*
> *THE PRIMORDIAL TRADITION*

Assignments

> Grof: *LSD: Doorway to the Numinous,* chapter 5, pages 157–217
>
> Tranche 2: Student BPM papers. Sign up for a slot.
>
> Recreational Internet Field Trip: Nichols, Dave. www.maps.org /news-letters/v09n4 [Click on "From Eleusis to PET Scans"] This is also a portal to back issues of the *MAPS Bulletin.* [From Vol. 9, No. 4, winter 1999/2000]

Sept. 30

Quote for Discussion

> *Deep reverence for life and ecological awareness are among the most frequent consequences of the psychospiritual transformation that accompanies responsible work with non-ordinary states of consciousness. The same has been true for spiritual emergence of a mystical nature that is based on personal experience. It is my belief that a movement in the direction of a fuller awareness of our unconscious minds will vastly increase our chances of planetary survival.*
>
> STANISLAV GROF, *THE HOLOTROPIC MIND*

Assignments

> Weekly Internet Field Trip: www.atpweb.org [Association for Transpersonal Psychology website]
>
> Grof: *LSD: Doorway to the Numinous,* chapter 6, pages 218–42
>
> Tranche 3: Student BPM papers. Sign up for a slot.

Oct. 2

Assignments

> Grof Test (a terrible BPM II and III experience)
>
> Recreational Internet Field Trip: www.ibogaine.org (site discontinued)

Oct. 7

Fig. App. A.1. Sciences involved in the study of LSD and other hallucinogens.
(From: Hintzen, Annelie and Torsten Passie, 2010.
The Pharmacology of LSD: A Critical Review. *Courtesy of*
Oxford University Press/Beckley Foundation Press, 7.)

Assignments

Roberts: *The Psychedelic Future of the Mind,* pages 1–36

Oct. 9

Quote for Discussion

> *The most important obligation of any science is that*
> *its descriptive and theoretical language embrace all the*
> *phenomena of its subject matter; the data from [altered*
> *states of consciousness] cannot be ignored if we are to have a*
> *comprehensive psychology.*

CHARLES T. TART

Assignments

Roberts: *The Psychedelic Future of the Mind,* pages 37–54

Recreational Internet Field Trip: http://blip.tv/mjhhaven
/psychedelic-4604065 (site discontinued) An hour+ lecture by
Roberts on psychedelics and spiritual growth, followed by questions and discussion.

Oct. 14

Assignments

Roberts: *The Psychedelic Future of the Mind,* pages 55–87

Weekly Internet Field Trip: www.drugpolicy.org [The Drug Policy
Alliance website] Explore this top policy site.

Oct. 16

Quote for Discussion

> *In recent years the West has begun to appreciate the fact
> that tribal societies can teach us much about the natural
> world from which we are so often alienated. It seems we
> may also have much to learn about the supernatural
> world, from which we are likewise alienated. Bearing
> in mind that humans have an innate need to experience
> altered states of consciousness, to ignore or repress our
> own natures in this way is to neglect our own capacities.
> What anthropology can do, by describing other cultures
> in which scientific and poetic approaches to truth are part
> of a holistic vision, is to remind us of the lack of harmony
> in the elements of our own second nature. It can indicate
> ways in which we may reach a better understanding of the
> importance of altered states of consciousness in both our
> collective and our personal lives.*

RICHARD RUDGLEY,
ESSENTIAL SUBSTANCES IN SOCIETY

Assignments

Roberts: *The Psychedelic Future of the Mind,* pages 88–117

Recreational Internet Field Trip: www.csp.org/communities
/docs/vaughan-balance.html (site discontinued) "A Question of
Balance: Health and Pathology in New Religious Movements."

Oct. 21

Quote for Discussion

> *It should not be necessary to supply any more proof that
> psychedelic drugs produce experiences that those who
> undergo them regard as religious in the fullest sense.*
>
> LESTER GRINSPOON AND JAMES BAKALAR,
> PSYCHEDELIC DRUGS RECONSIDERED

Assignments

Weekly Internet Field Trip: www.csp.org/chrestomathy (site discontinued) While there explore around the rest of the CSP website.
Roberts: *The Psychedelic Future of the Mind,* pages 119–45

Oct. 23

Quote for Discussion

> *There are a lot of people for whom psychedelics have been
> really beneficial. But I wouldn't recommend it to everyone.
> Some people are just not ready but society would benefit
> from letting people who are ready for psychedelics have
> legal access to them.*
>
> KARY MULLIS

Assignments

Roberts: *The Psychedelic Future of the Mind,* pages 146–76

Question: Who has the knowledge, right, power, or expertise to
decide religious issues having to do with the entheogenic uses of
psychedelics?

Recreational World Series Internet Field Trip. www.dockshort
.com/dockshort (site discontinued) Yes, it really happened.

Oct. 28

Quote for Discussion

> *At the point in his evolutionary progress where we first call
> him "Man" beyond a doubt—Homo sapiens sapiens—
> and when he came to know, also beyond a doubt, what
> awe and reverence were, he clearly felt that Soma was
> conferring on him mysterious sensations and powers, which
> seemed to him more than normal: at that point Religion
> was born, Religion pure and simple, free of Theology, free
> of Dogmatics, expressing itself in awe and reverence and
> in lowered voices, mostly at night, when people would
> gather together to consume the Sacred Element. The first
> entheogenic experience could have been the first, and an
> authentic, perhaps the only authentic miracle. This was the
> beginning of the Age of Entheogens, long, long ago.*
>
> WASSON ET AL., *PERSEPHONE'S QUEST*

Assignment

Weekly Internet Field Trip: www.druglibrary.org/schaffer/lsd
[Schaffer Library of Drug Policy Website] (a rich source)
Roberts: *The Psychedelic Future of the Mind*, pages 178–206

Oct. 30

Quote for Discussion

> *The experiment was powerful for me, and it left a
> permanent mark on my experienced worldview. (I say
> "experienced worldview" to distinguish it from what I
> think and believe the world is like.) For as long as I can
> remember I have believed in God, and I have experienced*

his presence both within the world and when the world was transcendentally eclipsed. But until the Good Friday Experiment, I had had no direct personal encounter with God of the sort bhakti yogis, Pentecostals, and born-again Christians describe. The Good Friday Experiment changed that, presumably because the service focused on God as incarnate in Christ.

HUSTON SMITH,
CLEANSING THE DOORS OF PERCEPTION

Assignment

Roberts: *The Psychedelic Future of the Mind,* pages 207–34
Recreational Internet Field Trip: www.beckleyfoundation.org [Beckley Foundation website]
In-class video: Halloween Special, *The Witch's Curse*

Nov. 4

Quote for Discussion

That's the essence of science: Ask the impertinent question, and you are on your way to pertinent science.

JACOB BRONOWSKI, *THE ASCENT OF MAN*

Assignment

Test: *The Psychedelic Future of the Mind*

Nov. 6

Quote for Discussion

Time, events, or the unaided individual action of the mind will sometimes undermine or destroy an opinion without any outward sign of change. . . . No conspiracy has been formed to make war on it, but its followers one by one noiselessly secede. As its opponents remain mute or only interchange their thoughts by stealth, they are themselves unaware for a long time that a great revolution has actually been effected.

ALEXIS DE TOCQUEVILLE

Assignments

Walsh and Grob: *Higher Wisdom,* pages 1–45

Recreational Internet Field Trip: www.dailymotion.com/video /x3snsc_the-bicycle-ride-by-david-normal_creation (3.5 mins.) ["The Bicycle Ride" by David Normal, posted by tribble423]

Nov. 11

Quote for Discussion

If the doors of perception were cleansed every thing would appear to man as it is, infinite.

WILLIAM BLAKE

Assignments

Weekly Internet Field Trip: www.cedu.niu.edu/lepf/edpsych /faculty/roberts/Why-Is-Bicycle-Day-April-19th.doc (site discontinued)

Walsh and Grob: *Higher Wisdom,* pages 46–83

Nov. 13

Quote for Discussion

It was fun, fun, fun. Where else could a red-blooded American lie, kill, cheat, and rape with the sanction of the all-highest?

GEORGE HUNTER WHITE, U.S. NARCOTICS OFFICER,
ACID DREAMS, PAGE 70C

Assignments

Walsh and Grob: *Higher Wisdom,* pages 84–117

Recreational Internet Field Trip: www.csp.org/practices/entheogens /docs/huxley-drugs.html (site discontinued) [Huxley: Drugs that Shape Men's Minds]

Nov. 18

Quote for Discussion

> *Turn on. Tune in. Drop out.*
>
> TIMOTHY LEARY

Assignments

Weekly Internet Field Trip: http://en.wikipedia.org/wiki /Timothy_Leary [Wikipedia entry on Timothy Leary]

Walsh and Grob: *Higher Wisdom,* pages 147–77

Nov. 20

Quote for Discussion

> *Some years ago I myself made some observations on this aspect of nitrous oxide intoxication, and reported them in print. One conclusion was forced upon my mind at that time, and my impression of its truth has ever since remained unshaken. It is our normal waking consciousness, rational consciousness as we call it, is but one special type of consciousness, whilst all about it, parted from it by the filmiest of screens, there lie potential forms of consciousness entirely different. We may go through life without suspecting their existence; but apply the requisite stimulus, and at a touch they are there in all their completeness, definite types of mentality which probably somewhere have their field of application and adaptation. No account of the universe in its totality can be final which leaves these other forms of consciousness quite discarded. How to regard them is the question—for they are so discontinuous with ordinary consciousness.*
>
> WILLIAM JAMES,
VARIETIES OF RELIGIOUS EXPERIENCE

Assignments

Weekly Internet Field Trip: http://psypressuk.com/category

/literary-reviews-2011-present [Psychedelic Book Review Archive at Psychedelic Press website]

Walsh and Grob: *Higher Wisdom,* pages 179–205

Nov. 25

Quote for Discussion

> *The rejection of any source of evidence is always treason to that ultimate rationalism which urges forward science and philosophy alike.*
>
> ALFRED NORTH WHITEHEAD

Assignments

Walsh and Grob: *Higher Wisdom,* pages 207–39

Recreational Internet Field Trip: http://en.wikipedia.org/wiki/The_Electric_Kool-Aid_Acid_Test [Wikipedia entry on *The Electric Kool-Aid Acid Test*]

Dec. 2

Quote for Discussion

> *I should say also that I consider Humanistic, Third force Psychology to be transitional, a preparation of a still "higher" Fourth Psychology, transpersonal, transhuman, centered in the cosmos rather than in human needs and interest, going beyond humanness, identity, self-actualization and the like.*
>
> ABRAHAM MASLOW, PREFACE TO
TOWARD A PSYCHOLOGY OF BEING, 2ND EDITION

Assignments

Weekly Internet Field Trip: http://en.wikipedia.org/wiki/Owsley_Stanley [Wikipedia entry on Stanley Owsley]

Walsh and Grob: *Higher Wisdom,* pages 241–55.

Dec. 4

Quote for Discussion

> *Deep reverence for life and ecological awareness are among the most frequent consequences of the psychospiritual transformation that accompanies responsible work with non-ordinary states of consciousness, The same has been true for spiritual emergence of a mystical nature that is based on personal experience. It is my belief that a movement in the direction of fuller awareness of our unconscious minds will vastly increase our chances of planetary survival.*

> STANISLAV GROF, *THE HOLOTROPIC MIND*

Assignments

Test on *Higher Wisdom*. The exact topic is still vague, but here are three working ideas.

1) From a list of quotations from *Higher Wisdom,* one will be selected. Explain it and elaborate on it by showing that psychedelics can be useful in understanding some aspect of our minds and/or lives.

2) From a list of quotations from *Higher Wisdom,* you will be asked to show how two of them enrich, inform, and relate to each other.

3) Select your own quotation from *Higher Wisdom,* and use it as a theme for an essay that includes ideas and/or information from this course.

Week of Dec. 8—Turn in Portfolios

In place of a final, you will turn in your portfolio during a brief, scheduled meeting with me during this week. Your portfolio will include your current research report, quizzes, BPM analysis, book review, your own presentation handouts, and anything else that portrays your work this semester.

Also include a statement that accurately describes the grade you think you deserve and why that is an appropriate grade. Consider how much work you have done, its quality, thoroughness of your preparation, class participation, and anything else that evaluates your work in this course. However, do not compare your work to others in this class.

Psychedelics Without Borders

Notes for a Business Prospectus

Certainly, one of the most important questions to ask about psychedelic-assisted psychotherapy is "What is the fastest way for the largest number of people to benefit?" Or, "What works in our society?" As we look around us and as we experience our lives, practically everything comes via corporate structure. In a real sense, corporations are the bones, ligaments, and muscles of today's world, and it's more efficient to use them than oppose them.

What are the fastest ways of raising the billions of dollars necessary to pay for the extensive costs of bringing psychedelic medicines to approval and to market? What kinds of organizations have already done this globally? Most of our current medicines and medical devices reach the greatest number of people via corporate structures. Not only our medicines but also the computer I'm using now, its programs, its attached devices, the chair I'm sitting on, my clothes, the tea in my mug, electricity, and so forth are widely distributed and quickly available via corporate structures.

Look at beer. Look at food. Look at clothes. Look at publishing. Look at music. Look at apps. Psychedelics can use the corporate system to spread throughout the world too. In this appendix, we'll take a look at one idea of what a psychedelic corporation could look like.

Do I mean that corporations are the only way to spread psychedelics' many benefits? Certainly not. A good analogy is the beer industry. There are large international brewers, national and regional ones, local breweries, and a booming craft-brewing industry. People can legally make their own brew at home. Beer drinkers can select what most appeals to them from an array of choices. Similarly, our food comes via everything from large international conglomerates to farmers' markets and grow-your-own practices. A full range of opportunities offers more than just one possibility and lets people choose their medicines—so to speak. Similarly, psychedelics would be most widely available to most people most quickly by being available via a broad range of routes while at the same time allowing people to maximize their own tastes and interests.

MAPS, the Multidisciplinary Association for Psychedelic Studies (an American organization working to raise awareness and understanding of psychedelic substances) deserves congratulations for their public benefit corporation, as do universities and medical school research centers, small treatment groups, and individual therapists. But to combine the fullest coverage with greatest personal choice, people need the full range of opportunities—pro bono, corporate entities, private groups, individual professional practices, Western medicine, and indigenous practices.

In addition to promoting efficiency, a company can also be primarily owned and largely influenced by pro bono groups. Companies don't have to be all and entirely "money grubbing." A balanced system of personal, pro bono, and public corporate psychedelic constituencies will help keep any one of them from getting out of hand and allow patients and clients to select the type of organization that suits them best.

Rightly or wrongly, some people who want to extend psychedelic psychotherapy and personal growth as widely as possible see corporate capital structures as undesirable, sleazy, and even evil. But there may be a way to combine a pro bono reality with capitalist structure. A possible unusual feature of this fictional offering could be the "charitable allotment." Purchasers of these shares at the underwriting would be required to donate half their purchases to a charity recognized as such by the United States Internal Revenue Service or by appropriate local, state, or national laws in the jurisdictions where purchasers reside.

When considering this requirement, purchasers of shares at the initial public offering may be referred to as "investor-donors." For example, if an investor-donor buys 200 shares, he or she must donate 100 shares to a recognized charity. These shares are fully registered and identical to all other units. Such gifts may qualify as a charitable donation for federal income tax purposes, but the Internal Revenue Service has not made a determination on this issue. Investor-donors should note this additional risk.

Investor-donors may select any charity or charities of their choice, such as a church, university, museum, community organization, pro bono group, or other legally recognized eleemosynary institution. A business can establish foundations to receive these and other donations should investor-donors so desire. The foundations are entirely separate from the company, and charters allow such foundations to fund a wide variety of health-related, educational, religious, scientific, civic, and other pro bono projects. In the context of psychedelic psychotherapy, these uses might include, but are not limited to, paying fees for treatment and services for people who cannot afford to pay for services. Although a company cannot give preference as to the charity that would receive shares, charitable allotments could be used to further psychedelic research, either through a psychedelic foundation or through organizations such as the Multidisciplinary Association for Psychedelic Studies, Usona Foundation, the Albert Hofmann Foundation, or the Heffter Research Institute. Foundations, hospitals, and colleges have common stock shares in their current endowments, why not shares of psychedelic companies? Additionally, as shareholders they would influence their companies' policies.

This fictional prospectus for a company named Psychedelics Without Borders will help you imagine how such a structure might emerge, what its functions might be (both for medical and personal growth), how it can raise the billions of dollars to fund research that leads to approval, and, perhaps even more important, how it results in the side benefits of recruiting the financial and eleemosynary communities to support psychedelics.

PROSPECTUS

PRELIMINARY PROSPECTUS

Psychedelics Without Borders
Incorporated in the State of Delaware

An offering of 100,000,000 shares of common stock at $20 each

Summary: Psychedelics Without Borders (PWB, or "the company") anticipates offering 100,000,000 shares of common stock on or about (date forthcoming).

The company's main business will be to establish and operate therapeutic and professional growth centers internationally; these centers will provide professionally guided psychedelic sessions. The company expects to provide two types of services: (1) psychedelic-assisted psychotherapy and (2) psychedelic-assisted professional development.

This will be the initial public offering for the company and may represent special risks (see "Regulatory Matters" on page 171). With the proceeds of this offering, the company expects to establish therapeutic centers and professional development centers. The therapeutic centers will consist of freestanding, self-contained centers for referral patients and on-grounds, in-house centers located at existing major mental health hospitals and centers. Centers offering professional development will provide services for clients who wish to enhance religious experience, creativity, personal growth, problem-solving, academic and scholarly research, and similar nontherapeutic purposes.

The company believes it has already identified several potential drug candidates as investigational new drugs, and furthermore, that while additional studies may be required to firmly establish their safety and efficacy, preliminary studies support both their safety and efficacy.

THE SECURITIES

This offering consists of 100,000,000 shares of common stock in Psychedelics Without Borders (PWB) at an anticipated price of $20 per share.

The securities offered herein represent equal shares of ownership in PWB and currently are not publicly traded, and there can be no assurance that a public market will develop, or if developed, there can be no assurance of market liquidity.

Trading Symbol

Psychedelics Without Borders has applied to the National Association of Securities Dealers Automated Quotation system (NASDAQ) to trade PWB stock under the symbol LSDD.

Possible Unusual Demand

In addition to the usual financial interest in initial public offerings in the health care industry, PWB believes that indications of interest in PWB stock at its initial public offering may be unusually strong because:

1) some potential investors have experienced psychedelic drugs themselves and believe they have benefited from doing so

2) some potential investors know people who have experienced psychedelic drugs and believe they have benefited from doing so

3) some potential investors are familiar with the findings of pilot and preliminary studies (see "Candidate Drugs" on page 171)

4) some potential investors assume that the processes of drug discovery and preliminary safety and efficacy testing are largely accomplished and will speed the development of PWB

5) during the process of due diligence, individual and institutional investors will examine the evidence for psychedelics' safety and efficacy and will judge them both safe and efficacious when used as specified as the company proposes

Additionally, PWB recognizes that this offering may attract an unusual amount of media publicity on the internet, television, and print media, thereby possibly increasing demand for its stock and adding to its volatility both up and down. Accordingly and depending on demand for the stock, market conditions, and other factors, the price per share, number of shares, or both may be adjusted either up or down. There is no guarantee that any or all of these expectations will be met.

Future Financing

Due to the unpredictable nature of the company's business, additional funding may be necessary in the future. This may be acquired through equity, loans, or both. Typically for companies such as PWB, other financings are undertaken as milestones in the company's plans are reached. There is no assurance that PWB will reach these milestones or that financing will be forthcoming in the future.

THE COMPANY

History

Psychedelics Without Borders (PWB), Inc. incorporated in the state of Delaware [day, month, year]. PWB has applied to the Food and Drug Administration to commence clinical trials of several drugs that PWB believes offer advantages as adjuncts to psychotherapy. PWB also believes that these drugs as used within the confines of the proposed sessions are effective methods of increasing professional development including, but not limited to, creativity and problem-solving, providing insights of value to academic and scientific researchers, enhancing primary religious experience, stimulating artistic works, and ways of exploring and developing the human mind. No assurance can be given that the candidate drugs will prove effective, and if they are, no assurance can be given that the FDA will approve their uses as anticipated by PWB.

Unlike most pharmaceutical companies, whose business is the manufacture and sale of pharmaceuticals, PWB's primary business will not consist of drug sales but will consist of the service of providing professionally guided psychedelic "sessions." PWB may derive some income from the manufacture and sale of its drugs, but this is expected to be incidental to the company's main business, and PWB expects to derive little, if any, profit from the manufacture and sale of drugs. The company's primary service will include screening and preparation for the sessions, the sessions, and follow-up procedures. These sessions may be for either therapeutic or professional development purposes.

Corporate Structure

Accordingly, the company's structure consists of two divisions, the psychedelic therapy division and the psychedelic professional development division. The company calls prospective purchasers of the services of the psychedelic therapy division "patients," and calls prospective purchasers of the services of the psychedelic professional development division "clients."

Therapy Centers	Professional Development Centers
alcoholism	spiritual development and religious studies
drug addiction	creativity and problem-solving
post-traumatic stress disorder	self-development and self-knowledge
depression	research and education
memory recovery	scholarly and academic
boosting immune system	mental health
neuroses and psychoses	scientific
hospice care	war/peace studies
training mental health professionals	aesthetic
sexual dysfunction	mapping human mind
obsessive-compulsive disorder	inventing new mindbody states
migraine and cluster headaches	constructing new cognitive processes
positive psychological health	

Depending on regulatory and other matters, the two divisions and their centers may be located in the same state or in different states of the same nation or in different nations. (See "Location" on page 173.) They may also be housed together or separately.

Psychedelic Therapy Division

The psychedelic therapy centers will provide services only to clients who are referred by mental health professionals who are certified or licensed in the jurisdictions where the centers are located. In the United States, these will vary from state to state. Internationally, these will vary from country to country. Officially recognized competent authorities are likely to include psychiatrists, clinical psychologists, and others similarly licensed or certified.

At the present, PWB believes its proposed therapeutic services have been shown by preliminary studies to be safe and efficacious for the following indications: alcoholism, drug addiction, post-traumatic stress disorder, lost memory recovery, depression, autism, and selected neurotic and psychotic diagnoses recognized in the *Diagnostic and Statistical Manual-IV.* Regulatory approval will require additional studies to establish these claims.

As experience with these drugs and PWB's method of running sessions increases, PWB believes that other indications will emerge. Among these is the possibility that intense, overwhelming self-transcendent experiences may boost the immune system. PWB believes that existing studies suggest this may be the case but that such evidence is not strong and that additional studies may or may not confirm these leads.

Current plans for the therapy centers call for some centers to be located in-house or on the grounds of existing mental health facilities such as state mental hospitals, private residential treatment centers, and similar locations. Other centers will be located as freestanding centers. PWB envisions freestanding centers located so as to serve the needs of several mental health facilities and professionals in an area.

PWB believes that psychedelic sessions also have value in the training of mental health professionals and will provide both pre-service and in-service education for these groups. PWB plans to apply to appropriate governmental agencies and/or educational accrediting agencies for permission to offer Continuing Education Units, "CEUs," for this training. In some cases these CEUs may be offered in conjunction with educational institutions such as medical schools, nursing schools, institutions of higher education, professional societies, and others. Here again, standards for national and local jurisdictions will need to be met.

While PWB believes that enough referrals will occur to make the psychedelic therapy centers profitable, no assurance can be given that this will be the case.

Psychedelic Professional Development Division

Psychedelic professional development centers will provide services for professional and vocational development in business, religion, education, scholarship, science, law, mental health, the arts, and related fields. Instead of being undertaken for the purpose of treating or curing an existing mental health condition, sessions of the professional development centers will be undertaken to work in the fields listed above. PWB believes the proposed services have been shown to be safe and efficacious, but PWB makes no assurance that regulatory agencies will interpret the existing studies this way. A major barrier to regulatory approval is the assumption that psychoactive substances have appropriate use only in medicine and psychotherapy. PWB may have to undertake, or cause to be undertaken, additional studies to provide evidence of the usefulness of psychedelic sessions for nonmedical purposes.

Because the proposed activities of the professional development centers are not medical or psychotherapeutic, it is not clear what governmental agencies, if any, have jurisdiction over these issues. This unresolved regulatory issue is especially acute for the religious, artistic, and educational uses because these areas have traditionally been outside U.S. government control. Pending the resolution of this issue, PWB believes that psychedelic professional development centers may first be established outside the United States.

Clients of the professional development division must be certified as at low risk of aversive consequences from their sessions, and, like the patients of the psychedelic therapy centers, they will undergo screening, preparation, the session itself, and post-session follow-up.

Some psychedelic professional development centers may be associated with a specific institution such as a major university, research facility, church, or monastery; others may serve consortia of institutions; and others may be associated with, or sponsored by, professional organizations. Professional development centers may be owned and operated by PWB or by autonomous individuals under license from PWB.

SESSIONS

Both therapeutic services and professional development services will consist of four phases: (1) screening, (2) preparation, (3) the session, and (4) post-session follow-up. Because these differ according to the nature of the patients and clients and the nature of the desired outcomes, the details of the procedures are only summarized here and need to be more fully worked out and described in a manual such as Mithoefer et al. *A Manual for MDMA-Assisted Psychotherapy in the Treatment of Posttraumatic Stress Disorder* (2017), which is incorporated herein by reference.

Screening consists of physical and psychological examinations to determine whether the applicant clients and patients are physically hardy enough to withstand possible stressful emotional and psychosomatic stress. Preparation consists of determining the client's/patient's personal preferences of setting and explaining to the client/patient the kinds of experiences he or she is likely to experience during the session, the activities that may occur (such as listening to music), and so forth. It will include establishing rapport with the guide or guides who will attend the patient/client during the session day. A typical session will take a full day. The client/patient will be administered the drug and will be accompanied throughout the session by at least one professional.

After a session, which may last twelve hours or more, clients and patients may stay overnight at the center or may be accompanied to their homes. In the case of patients in the therapy centers, who are residents at mental health treatment facilities, they will be returned to the custody of their institutions the same day, or they may stay overnight and return the next day. During the follow up, the session and its effects will be evaluated. In the case of patients, this activity will include the patients' doctor and/or therapist. In the case of clients of the professional development centers, the clients, as well as the session guide, will typically evaluate the outcome. Due to the nature of psychedelic sessions, the follow-up evaluations may include unanticipated results as well as the intended ones.

REGULATORY MATTERS

Candidate Drugs

The drugs that PWB plans to test and develop are psychoactive drugs commonly known as "psychedelic" or "hallucinogenic" drugs. These include, but are not limited to, LSD, DPT, DMT, MDA, MDMA, psilocybin, ayahuasca, ibogaine, and mescaline. Other compounds may be added from time to time. Currently these drugs are Schedule I drugs, meaning they are classified as having strong potential for abuse and no accepted medical value. PWB believes that this scheduling is in error and that these compounds should be listed as Schedule II drugs, meaning they have both recognized medical uses and recognized risks. PWB believes clinical trials have shown that these drugs have therapeutic value and can be used safely. PWB will have to expand these trials, including adding more controls. There can be no assurance that PWB will successfully show safety and efficacy, and if successful, there can be no assurance that the United States Food and Drug Administration will reclassify the drugs.

PWB believes that these drugs should not be prescribed to patients in such a way that the patients can buy them and self-administer them and that their proper use requires the presence of fully trained professionals, similar in this respect to the way anesthetics are currently administered, and patients may not take these substances home with them. PWB's business will be to provide screening and preparation for the pre-sessions, administration and guidance during the sessions, and follow-up after the sessions.

Drug Discovery

While most pharmaceutical companies and drug discovery companies spend much of their effort identifying new drug candidates, PWB believes that it has already identified potentially successful investigational new drug candidates, including those listed above. In PWB's view, this may eliminate or reduce both the expense of identifying potential drug candidates and the time needed to identify them; however, there is no assurance that these candidate drugs or any others yet to be discovered will be approved by relulatory agencies here or abroad.

Drug Testing and Approval

PWB also believes that Phase I safety and Phase II/III efficacy trials can be completed more quickly than is the case with most new investigational drugs because preliminary and pilot studies already indicate that these drugs can be safely used in an investigational capacity. Because appropriate federal agencies in the United States and in selected foreign countries have already granted some of these drugs the status of investigational new drugs, PWB believes that its applications for the same status will be approved expeditiously. Building on these pilot and preliminary studies, PWB plans to commence combined Phase I safety trials and Phase II trials to identify possible indications for psychedelic psychotherapy. Here too, PWB believes, preliminary investigations have already identified indications for psychedelics as psychotherapeutic adjuncts. Although PWB believes preliminary identification of investigational new drug candidates has already been achieved, that safety has already been demonstrated, and that pilot studies already indicate likely uses in psychotherapy, there can be no assurance that these goals have been met, and there can be no assurance that United States federal regulatory agencies will share PWB's opinions.

LOCATION

Long-term plans call for PWB to offer its services internationally. While PWB plans to establish psychedelic therapy centers and professional development centers first within the United States, then internationally, should the regulatory climate prove difficult in the United States and more favorable in other nations, this order may be reversed. PWB may even offer its services only in countries other than the United States. PWB will apply for approval by other governments to establish centers in their jurisdiction. This possibility includes but is not limited to countries in the European Common Market. Because of their histories of successful psychedelic psychotherapy and research, PWB believes that countries with more favorable regulatory climates include Switzerland, the Netherlands, Spain, Germany, Scandinavian countries, and the Czech Republic. Other countries may also be included, and PWB recognizes that Eastern European countries with a need for hard currencies may be especially willing to have PWB develop centers within their borders. These would be available for both nationals of the host countries and for nationals of other countries; the latter, especially if from hard-currency countries, would contribute to the economic development of the host countries.

OTHER MATTERS

Insurance and medical coverage: at this time these services are not covered by insurance payments or group health care plans. PWB hopes that as the safety and efficacy of PWB's services become established, insurance plans and similar health plans will add psychedelic sessions to their eligible treatments. There can be no assurance that they will do so, or if they do so, there can be no assurance that the entire cost of treatment will be covered.

FAQS

Are you kidding? This sounds like a good idea, but more of a pipe dream than a possibility.

If society is to benefit from psychedelics' potential, psychedelics have to be embedded in an acceptable activity and recognized institution that people know and trust. Psychedelics need to move to an "insiders" interest, not just something a few "outsiders" are toying with. At the present, people who are interested in using psychedelics, even carefully, are perceived as located on the fringes of society in this interest although not in all aspects. The question is, "How do we move the benefits from the fringes to the center?"

Founding a company to provide psychedelic-assisted psychotherapy is one way. Importantly, it's a way that people understand. It fits in with how people know society works, especially how many powerful people think about things. If stockholders are willing to "put their money where their mouth is," the idea gains credibility. A multimillion-dollar company (or even a billion-dollar company) that is willing to invest in psychedelics has more credibility than does an isolated research project here or a small treatment project there.

A multimillion-dollar company, or even a billion-dollar company? You must be kidding!

The numbers support it.

According to the *2009 National Survey on Drug Use and Health*, 23,600,000 Americans had used LSD. Another 14,200,000 had used MDMA; an unestimated number had used other hallucinogens. It is assumed that since then the numbers have increased; according to the 2006 survey, an additional 1.1 million hallucinogen users were added that year alone plus an additional 860,000 ecstasy users.

How many potential investors are there in PWB?

Even if we take a low-ball estimate of 1 percent of the 2009 LSD and MDMA numbers, do not count "other" hallucinogen users, and if we also omit any additional new users since then, that yields:

Potential Investors

$$
\begin{array}{r}
236,000 \text{ LSD users} \\
+ \quad 142,000 \text{ MDMA users} \\
\hline
378,000 \text{ TOTAL} \\
- \quad 71,000 \text{ estimated overlap @ ½ MDMA users} \\
\hline
307,000 \text{ estimated users}
\end{array}
$$

If each of the 307,000 estimated users invested an average of only $5,000 (another low-ball estimate), that would produce more than $1.5 billion (307,000 × $5,000 = $1,535,000,000). Most importantly, this estimate is only for the relatively small slice of the U.S. investment pie. We haven't added in the biggest pools of money, both individual and institutional:

- regular investors
- venture capitalists
- mutual funds
- banks
- insurance companies
- corporate retirement funds
- pension plans
- sovereign funds
- endowments
- and so forth

Unlike people who have used psychedelics, these groups aren't interested in psychedelics per se, much less in states of overwhelming unitive consciousness. They're interested in "Can PWB make money?" Or more accurately, "Can I make money by investing in PWB?" By appealing to the profit motive, this offering would inform these largely uninformed groups and recruit their support for responsible psychedelic use.

We haven't even considered foreign investors; these may well equal U.S. investors in their numbers. And wealthy domestic investors may want to invest substantial amounts. I have no idea how many of each of these there are, but a few large investors plus foreign investors could well lift an IPO to several billion.

The idea of going public is just too weird.

That's what people thought of a medical marijuana initial public offering in 2001. G. W. Pharmaceutical, Ltd., Britain's only legal marijuana producer, is selling a marijuana-derived medicine in Canada and Europe, and has FDA approvals in the United States for a first, lead product. G. W. Pharmaceutical, Ltd., increased its IPO to six times the amount they had originally planned on. The 2017–2018 cannabis stock boom indicates a shift of financial thinking. Can we expect something similar with psychedelics and PWB? No one knows, but this is an indication that risk-informed, mindapp-informed investors are out there and willing to invest.

OK, but can PWB make money?

This is *the* question, and we'll know that only after PWB is in business for a couple of years. But there are good reasons to think it can. We know the evidence so far shows that psychedelics used properly as adjuncts to psychotherapy and in safe clinical settings can be effective for treating the conditions listed for the therapy division. The exact dollars-and-cents figures and a sound business plan are one of the things PWB's founders will have to work out. In the long run, it clearly looks like this service will save money on psychotherapy treatment. Insurance companies and national health plans should like this benefit.

Wall Street is used to evaluating new technologies, products, services, and processes, and it seldom has as much evidence to start with as it does with psychedelics, and it seldom has as much preliminary research already accomplished as it does with PWB.

A big task now is building a business model.

*Due Diligence and Fiduciary Responsibility as Drug Education
for the Investment Community*

The question "Can PWB make money?" requires brokers, bankers, mutual fund managers, and others in the investment community to investigate this question. To answer it they'll have to read the research on psychedelics, obtain professional opinions from people who know the evidence, and generally "ask around." This is part of the process of due diligence, which is finding out what one can about a corporation before investing. While exercising due diligence for financial and fiduciary reasons, they will learn about pilot studies that have already been done. These are the accomplishments and leads psychedelically informed people already know about.

A significant effect of this stock offering will be to reach important, powerful, and influential parts of the public. The significance of informing these segments of society should not be underemphasized. In the process of looking for good investments, when exercising due diligence, and as a normal and necessary part of their professions, brokers, bankers, and investment managers of all types—people who would not normally be interested in psychedelic psychotherapy and psychedelic professional development—would learn about the benefits psychedelics can bring if they are used carefully. As well as raising money, a strong and accurate prospectus would educate some powerful people by summarizing the state of psychedelic research to date.

Additionally, therapists and others in psychedelic-related occupations have friends in the financial and business community's various branches who are psychedelically informed, so in a certain sense, parts of these communities are already favorably primed.

The financial and business communities, and through them the wider society, would become informed of psychedelics' potentials via this stock offering. This is no small accomplishment.

How long would it take PWB to reach significant milestones?
Actually, if you compare PWB to other startup pharmaceutical and biotech companies, PWB has already successfully passed some

developmental stages, and other stages appear to be just down the road. For example, searching for drug candidates takes years, many false starts, and lots of expensive screening. PWB already has a dozen or more candidates, so this milestone has been passed even before the company is formed.

Phase I, Safety

Furthermore, extensive research has already been done on many of these drug candidates, sometimes under the aegis of research on drugs of abuse and more recently by the movement of psychedelic research into the mainstream. Testing for safety and efficacy takes years more, and here too, PWB is advanced, as some of its candidates for investigational new drugs have already been tested for safety; federal agencies have approved some of them for medical research.

Phase II, Uses and Protocols

Work with, say, LSD done in the 1950s, '60s, and '70s has explored and identified various possible uses and treatment protocols. Some of this work would have to be replicated, but again, preliminary studies point the way to larger and more carefully controlled clinical studies, and current clinical research studies provide data about what works and how to increase effectiveness. To investors, this is all music to their ears: these already-completed and in-process tasks reduce PWB's expenses compared with other pharmaceutical startups and will likely speed up bringing PWB to profitability.

Phase III, Efficacy

Much of the money raised by this public offering will be used for Phase III efficacy studies. PWB is likely to fund research at medical research institutes, clinical project sites, and hospitals.

Other markers of progress include governmental approvals for various stages in research, development, production, and treatment. As noted, there is good reason to believe these will be forthcoming because of previous decisions. Here again, we are talking about approvals in both the United States and in other countries. Obtaining use patents is another range of systematic advances. Actually building the centers and starting treatment indicate progress, and so forth. To investors, the big advantage of PWB as an investment is that so much progress has already been achieved.

What about stockholder support for PWB and related drug policies?

This shouldn't be underestimated. It would help a lot to have, say, Chase Bank, Citicorp, Fidelity, Vanguard, Prudential, Merrill Lynch, Morgan Stanley, and so forth interested in PWB's welfare. These are powerful interests, and they are ones people take seriously. These organizations and substantial individual investors would, in effect, be part of the lobby too. For example, with XYZ National Bank and some of its major stockholders also being stockholders of PWB as well as contributors to political campaign funds, senators and representatives from XYZ's district are going to know where their interests lie. For legislators and regulators, it's one thing to have Dr. X, who has no political clout, apply for permission to do exploratory research on LSD and quite another to have a multimillion-dollar corporation with a network of powerful friends apply. Actually, PWB may very well fund Dr. X's research so that both can benefit.

Why a corporation? There are other ways of using psychedelics and benefiting from them too.

Yes, there are, and they should all be pursued. I'm not suggesting PWB as the only way, but one among others. A whole set of organizations is needed, and their very existence will support each other. These would include professional and scholarly organizations, foundations, educational programs, and so on.

One of the real advantages of a corporation is that it forms a structure for combining the interests and resources of many people into one coordinated effort. There is lots of good individual work centered around psychedelics, such as books being written and websites produced, and some small-group efforts such as conferences and publications, but a move to an international stage requires the cooperation and coordination of thousands of people. Not only does a stock corporation provide a way to collect and focus energy, but because it is potentially a profit-making entity, it can also recruit people who want to make money, along with their resources and support.

What about all the negative publicity? Wouldn't the word *psychedelic* scare away investors?
Publicity would likely come in three phases. First would be the immediate surprised, skeptical, and humorous reactions, with headlines like *The Sixties Reborn—Hey, Man, Want to Buy Some LSDD?, Heads Up on Wall Street, Market High on LSDD, Hippie Investment Vehicle.* This is to be expected; it will have the benefit of attracting attention, and it will die down when people examine the therapeutic potentials and PWB's financials and business plan.

The second phase would probably tone down the first with views like *LSD for Drunks? PWB Says It Dries Them Out, Investment Bankers Taking LSD—Seriously.* This phase would reflect people actually investigating the prospectus's claims.

The third phase? Perhaps this is more hope than actuality, but I think it's a realistic possibility: *Strong Indications Cause PWB to Raise Offering Price and Number of Shares, Today's IPOs: LSDD Takes Investors Higher.*

Now *I* have a question for *you*.
What do you think an LSDD stock certificate could look like?

Bicycle Day's Beginnings

Since 1985, some people have observed Bicycle Day on April 19th. This is the anniversary of the day that Albert Hofmann intentionally took LSD in 1943. On the 16th, Hofmann accidentally absorbed a bit of LSD, but the 19th was the first intentional experience, when he took what he then considered a minimum effective dose, 250 mcgs. In *LSD, My Problem Child* he records that day.

> By now it was already clear to me that LSD had been the cause of the remarkable experience of the previous Friday, for the altered perceptions were of the same type as before, only much more intense. I had to struggle to speak intelligibly. I asked my laboratory assistant, who was informed of the self-experiment, to escort me home. We went by bicycle, no automobile being available because of wartime restrictions on their use. On the way home, my condition began to assume threatening forms. Everything in my field of vision wavered and was distorted as if seen in a curved mirror. I also had the sensation of being unable to move from the spot. Nevertheless, my assistant later told me we had traveled very rapidly.

In this dark hour of ignorance and superstition about psychedelics, you can light a candle of hope and reason. To commemorate the bicycle ride that changed the world forever, let's celebrate Bicycle Day with bicycle trips, by sending cards with bicycle pictures on them to friends, or with joyful picnics and other festive activities.

Remember Bicycle Day and Keep It Holy

Fig. App.C.1. Bicycle Day

WHY IS BICYCLE DAY APRIL 19TH, NOT THE 16TH?

As I recall, I originally wanted to celebrate the 16th, but in 1985 the 16th was midweek and not a good day for a party, and the 19th was on a weekend, so I decided to celebrate the first *intentional* LSD exposure instead of Hofmann's first exposure on the 16th. Had the calendar been different, the 16th would have been Bicycle Day. It seems to me that the discovery of LSD deserves two dates, so maybe someone will start a Hofmann Day or LSD Discovery Day event.

After several years of celebrations, I had Bicycle Day embroidered cloth patches made. The first is 1991. One of my former students made the announcement letter for the 1993 celebration that I've sent out since then. Of course, others might have celebrated that date before me (or they might have preferred the 16th as I did originally), but I made up the name "Bicycle Day."

Some years ago Albert and I corresponded about why I paid attention to the bicycle instead of calling it "LSD Day" or something similar. I told him that the bicycle was a more concrete image than a chemical structure, and in America there is a famous poem by Henry Wadsworth Longfellow that marks the start of our revolution in 1775. It has a parallel with his ride. It begins:

> *Listen, my children, and you shall hear*
> *Of the midnight ride of Paul Revere,*
> *On the eighteenth of April, in Seventy-five;*
> *Hardly a man is now alive*
> *Who remembers that famous day and year*

American schoolchildren used to memorize this poem. The Hofmann ride and the Revere ride are analogous, each marking the beginning of a new era. To the people invited to my party, the parallels would be naturally apparent.

That's why the celebration and name got attached to the 19th, not the 16th.

Notes

CHAPTER 1. A SCENT OF PORTENT

1. **wiser but less cocksure.** Huxley, *The Doors of Perception,* 79.
2. **behaviorism.** B. F. Skinner, *Cumulative Record* (Boston: Appleton-Century Crofts, 1959).
3. ***Summerhill.*** A. S. Neill, *Summerhill: A Radical Approach to Child Rearing* (New York: Hart Publishing, 1962).
4. **Maslow's needs hierarchy.** Abraham H. Maslow, *Motivation and Personality* (New York: Harper & Row, 1954).
5. **my doctoral dissertation.** Thomas B. Roberts, "A Humanistic Social Typology with Applications to a Study of Higher Education and Suggestions for a Social Theory" (unpublished doctoral dissertation, Stanford University, 1972).
6. **Willis Harman.** "Willis Harman," Wikipedia.
7. **San Francisco acid scene.** Elizabeth Gips and Evan Sandler, *The Scrapbook of a Haight Ashbury Pilgrim: Spirit, Sacraments & Sex in 1967–68* (Santa Cruz, Calif.: Changes Press, 1995).
8. **media-hype.** Siff, *Acid Hype.*
9. **novelty-seeking.** R. Cloniger, *The Temperament and Character Inventory (TCI): A Guide to its Development and Use* (St. Louis, Mo.: Washington University Center for Psychobiology of Personality, 1994).
10. **Esalen Institute.** "Esalen Institute," Wikipedia.
11. **Alan Watts.** "Alan Watts," Wikipedia.
12. **self-actualization.** Maslow, *Farther Reaches,* 41–58; Roberts, *The Psychedelic Future of the Mind,* 33–36.

13. **Maslow was interested in LSD.** Maslow, *Farther Reaches,* 42, 108, 159, 218, 389.

14. **[Maslow was interested in the] work of Stanislav Grof.** Maslow, *Farther Reaches,* 411. See also Abraham H. Maslow, *Religions, Values, and Peak-Experiences* (New York: Penguin, 1970), xiv.

15. **Bïfrost [Iceland conference].** G. Vilhjalmsson and T. Weide, "The First International Transpersonal Conference," *The Journal of Transpersonal Psychology* 5, no. 1 (1973): 55–61.

16. **Walter H. Clark.** Wolfgang Saxon, "Walter Clark, 92; Taught Psychology of Religion," *New York Times,* 1994 archive online.

17. *The Psychology of Religion.* Walter Houston Clark, *The Psychology of Religion* (New York: Macmillan, 1958).

18. **the Good Friday Experiment.** Rick Doblin, "Pahnke's 'Good Friday Experiment': A Long-Term Follow-up and Methodological Critique," *The Journal of Transpersonal Psychology* 23, no. 1 (2014): 1–28.

19. *Chemical Ecstasy: Psychedelic Drugs and Religion.* Walter Houston Clark, *Chemical Ecstasy: Psychedelic Drugs and Religion* (New York: Sheed and Ward, 1969).

20. **Joseph Campbell.** "About Joseph Campbell," Joseph Campbell Foundation website.

21. *The Hero with a Thousand Faces.* Campbell, *The Hero with a Thousand Faces.*

22. **Huston Smith.** Douglas Martin and Dennis Hevesit, "Huston Smith, Author of 'The World's Religions,' Dies at 97," *New York Times,* January 1, 2017.

23. *The Religions of Man.* Huston Smith, *The Religions of Man* (San Francisco: Harper, 1958). Republished in 1991 as *The World's Religions.*

24. **Smith had pursued and retrieved the [*Good Friday Experiment*] participant.** Thomas B. Roberts and R. Jesse, "Recollections of the Good Friday Experiment: An Interview with Huston Smith," *The Journal of Transpersonal Psychology* 29, no. 2 (1997): 99–104.

25. *Cleansing the Doors of Perception: The Religious Significance of Entheogenic Plants and Chemicals.* Smith, *Cleansing the Doors of Perception.*

26. **Stanislav Grof.** "Stan Grof," website of Stanislav Grof, 2017.

27. **Four general reports.** (1) James Fadiman, "The Council Grove Conference on Altered States of Consciousness," *Journal of Humanistic Psychology* 9, (1969): 135–37. (2) James Fadiman, "The Second Council Grove Conference on Altered States of Consciousness," *The Journal of Transpersonal*

Psychology 2, (1970): 169–74. (3) T. Weide, "Council Grove III: The Third Annual Interdisciplinary Conference on the Voluntary Control of Internal States," *The Journal of Transpersonal Psychology* 3, (1971): 141–43. (4) T. Weide, "Council Grove IV—Toward a Science Concerned with Ultimates," *The Journal of Transpersonal Psychology* 4, no. 1, (1972): 81–83.

28. **Elmer and Alyce Green.** Elmer and Alyce Green, *Beyond Biofeedback* (New York: Delacorte Press, 1977).

29. **International Transpersonal Association.** "History," International Transpersonal Association website, 2018.

30. **420.** "420 (cannabis culture)," Wikipedia.

31. **"Consciousness Criticism."** Thomas B. Roberts, "Consciousness Criticism," *The CEA Critic* 44, no. 1 (1981): 15–32.

32. *Psychedelic Reflections.* Grinspoon and Bakalar, *Psychedelic Reflections.*

33. **first letter.** Thomas B. Roberts, "Letter from Prof. Tom Roberts, requesting scheduling hearing, August 13, 1984." MAPS website.

34. **An opinion piece.** Drug Policy Alliance and the Multidisciplinary Association for Psychedelic Studies, "The DEA: Four Decades of Impeding and Rejecting Science," in Ellens and Roberts, eds., *The Psychedelic Policy Quagmire.*

35. **Bicycle Day.** Thomas B. Roberts, "Why Is Bicycle Day April 19?" and "Bicycle Day Announcement," Academia website, 2018. See also appendix C of this book.

36. *Brainstorm.* Roberts, "Brainstorm," 126–36.

37. *Snow White.* Thomas B. Roberts, "A Grofian Interpretation of Walt Disney's Imagery in 'Snow White and the Seven Dwarfs,'" in A. Akhter, A. Doland, and C. Jordan, eds., *Handbook of Imagery Research and Practice* (Yonkers, N.Y.: Brandon House, 1987).

38. **Multistate Education.** Thomas B. Roberts, "Multistate Education: Metacognitive Implications of the Mindbody Psychotechnologies," *The Journal of Transpersonal Psychology* 21, no. 1 (1989): 83–102.

39. **paradigm shift.** Kuhn, *Scientific Revolutions.*

40. **drug policies.** Ellens and Roberts, eds., *The Psychedelic Policy Quagmire.*

CHAPTER 2. AUGMENTING HUMAN INTELLECT WITH MINDAPPS

1. **insulate a community.** Kuhn, *Scientific Revolutions,* 37.
2. **attitude of pseudoscience.** Ben Sessa, "The 21st Century Psychedelic

Renaissance: Heroic Steps Forward on the Back of an Elephant," *Psychopharmacology* 235, no. 2 (2018): 551.

3. **favorites.** Beckley Foundation website; Council on Spiritual Practices website; Erowid website; Heffter Research Institute website; Imperial College Psychedelic Research Group website; Multidisciplinary Association for Psychedelic Studies website; Núcleo de Estudos Interdisciplinares sobre Psicoativos website.

4. **resolve some outstanding and generally recognized problem[s].** Kuhn, *Scientific Revolutions,* 168.

5. **folk craft.** Alexandra Jacopetti and Jerry Wainwright, *Native Funk & Flash: An Emerging Folk Art* (San Francisco: Scrimshaw Press, 1974).

6. **art.** Ken Johnson, *Are You Experienced? How Psychedelic Consciousness Transformed Modern Art* (Munich: Prestel, 2011).

7. **design.** Alastair Gordon, *Spaced Out: Radical Environments of the Psychedelic Sixties* (New York: Rizzoli, 2008).

8. **music.** Nicholas Knowles Bromell, *Tomorrow Never Knows: Rock and Psychedelics in the 1960s* (New York: Seven Stories Press, 2000).

9. **microdosing.** Waldman, *A Really Good Day;* Olivia Solon, "Under Pressure."

10. **psychedelic creative problem-solving.** Fadiman, *The Psychedelic Explorer's Guide.*

11. **raise values and moral development.** Earp, "Psychedelic Moral Enhancement."

12. **open-mindedness.** MacLean, Johnson, and Griffiths, "Mystical Experiences Occasioned by the Hallucinogen Psilocybin Lead to increases in the Personality Domain of Openness," 1453–61.

13. *The Psychedelic Renaissance.* Sessa. *The Psychedelic Renaissance.*

14. **promise to preserve.** Kuhn, *Scientific Revolutions,* 168.

15. **altered states of consciousness.** Tart, *States of Consciousness.*

16. **mental self-management.** Sternberg, *The Triarchic Mind,* 72.

17. **increased power and energy of brain states.** Selene Atasoy, et al., "Connectome-harmonic Decomposition of Human Brain Activity Reveals Dynamical Repertoire Re-organization under LSD," *Nature, Scientific Reports 7,* article number 17661 (2017).

18. **metaintelligence.** Roberts, *Psychedelic Horizons,* 129–30.

19. **mindapps.** Ellens and Roberts, eds., *The Psychedelic Policy Quagmire,* 247–57.

20. **Mind & Brain News.** "Mind & Brain News" page on *ScienceDaily.*

21. **how cognitive psychology and ayahuasca can inform each other.** Shanon, *Antipodes*.

22. **mindbody states, anomalies.** Luke, *Otherworlds;* Rothen et al., "Coordinated Neural, Behavioral, and Phenomenological Changes in Perceptual Plasticity," 151–62.

23. **normal puzzle solving.** Kuhn, *Scientific Revolutions,* 35–42.

24. **"Do Psychedelic-induced Mystical Experiences Boost the Immune System?"** Roberts, *Psychedelic Future of the Mind.*

CHAPTER 3. MIND DESIGN

1. **brain must have changed.** American Friends of Tel Aviv University, "Cultural Activities May Influence the Way We Think: A New Model May Explain How Culture Helped Shape Human Cognition and Memory," *ScienceDaily* (Aug. 4, 2017): 1.

2. **best practices model.** Johnson, Richards, and Griffiths, "Human Hallucinogen Research," 603–20.

3. **problems of policy and practice.** Ellens and Roberts, eds., *The Psychedelic Policy Quagmire.*

4. **the Serotonin Club.** Nichols, "(1990–2000) From Eleusis to PET Scans," 50–55.

5. **when paradigms change.** Kuhn, *Scientific Revolutions,* 110.

CHAPTER 4. MINDAPPS FOR THE SCIENCES

1. **consilience.** Wilson, *Consilience,* 8.

2. **"to unite the natural sciences with the social sciences and humanities."** Wilson, *Consilience,* 267.

3. **ayahuasca as a clue.** Wilson, *Consilience,* 72.

4. **experiments in medical schools.** Council on Spiritual Practices website, "Psilocybin Research" (2018); Imperial College Psychedelic Research Group website, "Our Research" (2018).

5. **the hard problem.** Chalmers, "Facing Up to the Problem of Consciousness," 200–19.

6. **Benny Shanon's work with ayahuasca.** Shanon, *Antipodes.*

7. **changes in thinking that singlestate mind studies miss.** Shanon, *Antipodes,* 198–206.

8. **a two-way interaction.** Shanon, *Antipodes,* 37.

9. **anomalous.** Kuhn, *The Structure of Scientific Revolutions,* 52–65.

10. **synesthesia.** Devin B. Terhune, David Luke, and Roi Cohen Kadosh, "The Induction of Synaesthesia with Chemical Agents: A Systematic Review," *Frontiers in Psychology* 4 (2013): 753.

11. **to teach synesthesia.** Rothen et al., "Coordinated Neural, Behavioral, and Phenomenological Changes in Perceptual Plasticity," 151–62.

12. **birth memories and transpersonal experiences.** Grof, *LSD: Doorway to the Numinous,* 95–214.

13. *Psychedelics and Exceptional Human Experience.* Luke, *Otherworlds.*

14. **crises.** Kuhn, *Scientific Revolutions,* 77.

15. **one instrument which every discipline uses.** Lawrence S. Kubie, "The Forgotten Man of Education," *Harvard Alumni Bulletin* 56 (1954): 349–53.

16. **amplifier of unconscious mental processes.** Richard Yensen and Donna A. Dryer, "The Consciousness Research of Stanislav Grof: Cosmic Portal Beyond Individuality" (1998), 2.

17. **open-mindedness increased.** MacLean, Johnson, and Griffiths, "Mystical Experiences Lead to Increases in the Personality Domain of Openness," 1453–61.

18. **standard personality instrument.** John M. Digman, "Personality Structure: Emergence of the Five-factor Model," *Annual Review of Psychology* 41 (1990): 417–40.

19. **personality traits are relatively enduring.** MacLean, Johnson, and Griffiths "Mystical Experiences Lead to Increases in the Personality Domain of Openness," 1454.

20. **enhance creative problem-solving ability.** Harman et al., "Psychedelic Agents in Creative Problem Solving," 211–27.

21. **concrete evidence of enhancement.** Fadiman, *The Psychedelic Explorer's Guide,* 123.

22. *intelligence* **as "the ability to solve problems or produce goods . . ."** Howard Gardner, *Frames of Mind: The Theory of Multiple Intelligences* (New York: Basic Books, 1969), xxvii.

23. **microdosing.** Waldman, *A Really Good Day.*

24. **businesspeople and technology professionals.** Solon, "Under Pressure."

25. **connectome.** "Connectome," Wikipedia.

26. **adds communication networks within human brains.** Petri et al.,

"Homological Scaffolds of Brain Functional Networks," *Journal of the Royal Society Interface* 11 (2014): 101.

27. **flow of information between brain regions.** Goethe University as cited on, "Smart People Have Better Connected Brains: In Intelligent Persons, Some Brain Regions Interact More Closely, While Others De-couple Themselves," *ScienceDaily* (November, 22, 2017): 1.

28. **cognitively challenging.** Goethe University as cited on "Smart People Have Better Connected Brains," 2–3.

29. **brain imaging and mapping technique.** Jacob Seidlitz et al., "Morphometric Similarity Networks Detect Microscale Cortical Organisation and Predict Inter-individual Cognitive Variation," *Neuron* (December 21, 2017).

30. **relationship between connectivity and IQ.** University of Cambridge, "New Brain Mapping Technique Highlights Relationship Between Connectivity and IQ" (2017).

31. **perception of significance.** Ido Hartogshen. "The Meaning-Enhancing Properties of Psychedelics and Their Mediator Role in Psychedelic Therapy, Spirituality, and Creativity." *Frontiers in Neurosceince* 12, no. 129 (2018): 1.

32. **The Neurosingularity Project.** Ellens and Roberts, eds., *The Psychedelic Policy Quagmire,* 157–265.

CHAPTER 5. LAYERS OF MEANING

1. **psychological undercurrents that govern our experiences.** Grof, *LSD Psychotherapy* (2001), 299.

2. **carried psychedelics forward during years of neglect and oppression.** "Stanislav Grof," Wikipedia.

3. **low-dose or *psycholytic.*** Grof, *LSD Psychotherapy* (1980), 31.

4. **high-dose peak-experience psychedelic psychotherapy.** Grof, *LSD Psychotherapy* (1980), 32.

5. **methods that are generally used today.** Johnson, Richards, and Griffiths, "Human Hallucinogen Research," 603–19.

6. **Grof's four-level map of our minds.** Grof, *Realms of the Human Unconscious: Observations from LSD Research.* Republished in 2009 as *LSD: Doorway to the Numinous* in Rochester, Vt. by Park Street Press.

7. **vaster panoply of human experience.** Walsh and Grob, eds., *Higher Wisdom,* 118.

8. **outlooks of tribes, societies, civilizations.** Smith, *Forgotten Truth,* iv.

9. **the most formidable evidence the psychedelics have thus far produced.** Smith, *Forgotten Truth,* 156.

10. **reality that results is so uncannily.** Smith, *Forgotten Truth.*

11. **they [religions] are influenced by those stages.** Smith, *Forgotten Truth,* 89.

12. **entheogenic field of inquiry.** Ellens, ed., *Seeking the Sacred.*

13. ***Realms of the Human Unconscious.*** Grof, *Realms of the Human Unconscious.* Republished in 2009 as *LSD: Doorway to the Numinous.*

14. **search of our inward sea.** Campbell, *Myths to Live By,* 258.

15. **It is these [perinatal stages] that are represented in myth.** Campbell, *Myths to Live By,* 264.

16. **The passage of the mythological hero.** Campbell, *The Hero with a Thousand Faces,* 29.

17. **"adventure of the discovery of the self."** Campbell, *The Hero with a Thousand Faces,* 8.

18. **four-level Grofian psychocriticism.** Thomas B. Roberts, "The Mindbody Explorer as Hero and Grofian Film Criticism (slide lecture)," (2013), Available on Academia website.

19. **what's behind these cold eyes.** Waters, Appleby, and Scarfe, *Pink Floyd: The Wall,* unnumbered pages.

20. ***Brainstorm.*** Roberts, "Brainstorm," 126–36.

21. ***Snow White.*** Thomas B. Roberts, "Disney's Intrapsychic Drama—*Snow White and the Seven Dwarfs*—A Grofian Interpretation," *Psychedelic Monographs and Essays* 5, (1990): 19–41. See also Roberts, "Snow White," "Immune System," "Multistate Psychology," and "Enlarging Education," in *Psychedelic Horizons,* 17–44.

22. ***Fight Club.*** Hayal Kackar and Thomas B. Roberts, "*Fight Club* and the Basic Perinatal Matrices: A Movie Analysis via a Grofian Frame," *The Journal of Transpersonal Psychology* 37, no. 1 (2005): 44–51.

23. **political and military leaders use perinatal imagery.** Grof, "Perinatal Roots," 269–308.

24. **Hitler.** Grof, "Perinatal Roots."

25. **H. R. Giger as a master of BPM II.** Stanislav Grof, *Modern Consciousness Research and the Understanding of Art, Including the Visionary World of H. R. Giger* (Santa Cruz, Calif.: Multidisciplinary Association for Psychedelic Studies, 2015).

26. **images of dying and transcendence cross culturally.** Stanislav Grof and Christina Grof, *Beyond Death: The Gates of Consciousness* (London: Thames and Hudson, 1980).

27. **positively oriented scientists and skeptics and cynics, and uncompromising atheists.** Grof, *Realms of the Human Unconscious.* Republished in 2009 as *LSD: Doorway to the Numinous.*

28. **perinatal elements in the Gettysburg Address.** Mark B. Ryan, "Transpersonal Psychology and the Interpretation of History: A Reading of the Gettysburg Address," *The Journal of Transpersonal Psychology* 36, no. 1 (2004): 1–17.

29. **sixty-one drawings by Sherana Harriette Frances document the inner psychedelic journey.** Sherana Harriette Frances, *Drawing It Out: Befriending the Unconscious* (Sarasota, Fla.: Multidisciplinary Association for Psychedelic Studies, 2001).

30. **Sartre's mescaline experience.** Thomas J. Riedlinger, "Sartre's Rite of Passage," 105–23.

31. **pivotal area for major philosophical and intellectual issues.** Richard Tarnas, *The Passion of the Western Mind: Understanding the Ideas that Have Shaped our World View* (New York: Ballantine Books, 1993), 428.

CHAPTER 6. SAVE THE HUMANITIES!

1. **report that bemoaned the sorry state of the humanities.** American Academy of Arts and Sciences, *The Heart of the Matter: A Report of The Commission on the Humanities and Social Sciences* (2013).

2. **Psychedelic Renaissance.** Sessa, *The Psychedelic Renaissance.*

3. **recognized in general periodicals and online.** Pollan, "The Trip Treatment," 36–47; Alexandra Sifferlin, "Do LSD and Magic Mushrooms Have a Place in Medicine?" *Time* (May 26, 2015); Earth Erowid, "LSD-25," The Vaults of Erowid website (2016).

4. **museum exhibitions.** Sally Tomlinson and Walter Patrick Medeiros, *High Societies: Psychedelic Rock Posters of Haight Ashbury* (San Diego: San Diego Museum of Art, 2001).

5. **psychedelic aesthetic sensibility.** David Rubin, *Psychedelic: Optical and Visionary Art Since the 1960s* (Cambridge, Mass.: MIT Press, 2010), 16.

6. **spacey sounds, a trippy feel sometimes including Eastern influences and instruments.** Phil Hebblethwaite, "Are These the Most Psychedelic

Pieces of Classical Music?" BBC Music website (March 22, 2018).

7. **research-rich topics.** Griffiths et al., "Mystical-type Experiences Occasioned by Psilocybin Mediate the Attribution of Personal Meaning and Spiritual Significance 14 Months Later," 626.

8. *Persisting Effects Questionnaire.* To learn more about this study and the questionnaire, visit John F. Kihlstrom's home page on Berekely's Open Content site, then navigate to "Psychedelics" and "Psychedelics and Other Drug States," last revised September 17, 2018.

9. **creativity.** M. Baggott, "Psychedelics and Creativity: A Review of the Quantitative Literature," *Semantic Scholar* (2015).

10. **language for semiotic analysis.** Thomas C. Swift et al., "Cancer at the Dinner Table: Experiences of Psilocybin-Assisted Psychotherapy for the Treatment of Cancer-Related Distress," *Journal of Humanistic Psychology* 57, no. 5 (2017): 488–519.

11. **Romantic Science and Poetry.** Neşe Devenot, "Medical Ecstasies: Chemical Synthesis and Self-Experimentation in Romantic Science and Poetry," *European Romantic Review.*

12. **transform how we read canonical Romantic poetry.** Neşe Devenot (2017) Presentation, "Aldous Huxley's New Romanticisms: Reading Blake And Wordsworth After Mescaline." Uploaded to youtube by Breaking Convention on September 12, 2017.

13. *"THE EXPLODING THREAT OF THE MIND DRUG THAT GOT OUT OF CONTROL LSD."* A. Rosenfeld and B. Farrell, "A Remarkable Mind Drugs Suddenly Spells Danger LSD," *Life* 69, no. 12 (1966): 28–33, 30A–30D.

14. **"THE HIDDEN EVILS OF LSD."** Bill Davidson, "The Hidden Evils of LSD," *The Saturday Evening Post* 240, no. 16 (August 12, 1967): 19–23.

15. *Acid Hype.* Siff, *Acid Hype.*

16. **a list of 104 news reports.** M. Haden (2018) personal communication.

17. *The Psychedelic Policy Quagmire.* Ellens and Roberts, *The Psychedelic Policy Quagmire.*

18. **vast anthropological literature.** "Anthropology of Consciousness," Wikipedia.

19. *Sisters of the Extreme.* Cynthia Palmer and Michael Horowitz, *Sisters of the Extreme: Women's Writings on the Drug Experience* (Rochester, Vt.: Park Street Press, 2000).

20. ***Exploring Inner Space.*** Jane Dunlap, *Exploring Inner Space: Personal Experiences Under LSD-25* (New York: Harcourt, Brace & World, 1961).

21. ***My Self and I.*** Constance Newland, *Myself and I* (New York: Coward McCann, 1962).

22. **Black experience is now open a crack.** Nicholas Powers, "Which Black People Are Allowed to Trip?" *The Huffington Post,* March 12, 2018.

23. **"Black Masks, Rainbow Bodies: Race and Psychedelics."** Nicholas Powers, "Black Masks, Rainbow Bodies: Race and Psychedelics," presentation at *Horizons: Perspectives on Psychedelics,* New York City (2017). Video available on vimeo.

24. **Detroit Psychedelic Community.** To find out more about the annual Detroit Psychedelic Conference, please see the MAPS website or follow the Detroit Psychedelic Community on Facebook.

25. ***The Apples of Apollo.*** Carl Ruck, Blaise D. Staples, and Clark Heinrich, *The Apples of Apollo: Pagan and Christian Mysteries of the Eucharist* (Durham, N.C.: Carolina Academic Press, 2001).

26. **Pythia of Delphi.** L. Piccardi et al., "Scent of a Myth: Tectonics, Geochemistry, and Geomythology at Delphi (Greece)," *Journal of the Geological Society* 165, no. 1 (2008): 1–5.

27. ***The Chemial Muse.*** D. C. A. Hillman, *The Chemical Muse: Drug Use ad the Roots of Western Civilization* (New York: St. Martin's Press, 2008).

28. ***Essential Substances.*** Rudgley, *Essential Substances.*

29. **Psychoactive Plant Use in the Old World.** Merlin, "Archaeological Evidence for the Tradition of Psychoactive Plant Use in the Old World," 295–323.

30. **totalitarian governments.** Aldous Huxley, *Brave New World* (Garden City, N.Y.: Sun Dial Press, 1932).

31. **future themes in psychedelia's scholarly neighborhood.** Huxley, *Doors of Perception.*

32. **Mind at Large.** Huxley, *Doors of Perception,* 73.

33. **deliver us, dear God, from beliefs.** Huxley, *Island,* 101.

34. **mind-altering plants and chemicals have played in human history.** Smith, *Cleansing the Doors of Perception,* xv.

35. **spark that ignited the psychedelic culture.** Wasson, "Seeking the Magic Mushroom," 100–120.

36. **leading rock stars.** Michael Horowitz, "Collecting Wasson," in Riedlinger, ed., *The Sacred Mushroom Seeker,* 131.

37. **"Drugs that Shape Men's Minds."** Aldous Huxley, "Drugs that Shape Men's Minds," *The Saturday Evening Post* (October 18, 1958), 28–29, 106, 110–13.

38. **ninety-seven Wasson publications.** J. Christopher Brown, "Appendix II: Bibliography: R. Gordon Wasson and Valentina Pavlovna Wasson," in Riedlinger, ed., *The Sacred Mushroom Seeker,* 257–64.

39. **intoxicating mushrooms among the Indians in Mexico.** J. Christopher Brown, "R. Gordon Wasson: Brief Biography and Personal Appreciation," in Riedlinger, ed., *The Sacred Mushroom Seeker,* 19–24.

40. **"I Ate the Sacred Mushrooms."** Valentina Wasson, "I Ate the Sacred Mushrooms," *This Week* (May 19, 1957): 8–10, 36.

41. **I'd make mycoenthnology my trade.** Robert Graves in Paul O'Prey, ed., *Between Moon and Moon: Selected Letters of Robert Graves, 1946–1972* (Mount Kisco, N.Y.: Moyer Bell Limited, 1990), 216.

42. **Four of Graves's books.** Robert Graves, *Food for Centaurs* (Garden City, N.Y.: Doubleday & Co., 1962); *Oxford Addresses on Poetry* (Garden City, N.Y.: Doubleday & Co., 1973); *Difficult Questions, Easy Answers* (Garden City, N.Y.: Doubleday & Co., 1990); *Between Moon and Moon: Selected Letters of Robert Graves, 1946–1972.* Paul O'Prey, ed. (Mount Kisco, N.Y.: Moyer Bell Limited, 1990).

43. **Society for the Study of Consciousness.** SAC publishes a journal, *Anthropology of Consciousness;* holds an annual Spring Meeting; and sponsors sessions at other meetings, such as those of the American Anthropological Association (AAA). Through this site, SAC hopes to further scholarly exchanges between anthropologists and persons in other disciplines within consciousness studies.

44. *Intoxicants in Society.* Rudgley, *Essential Substances.*

45. **Psychoactive Plant Use in the Old World.** Merlin, "Archaeological Evidence for the Tradition of Psychoactive Plant Use in the Old World," 295–323.

46. **Ayahuasca.** An active ongoing source is the organization Chacruna. Please visit their website.

47. **A War on Intellect.** Ellens and Roberts, eds., *The Psychedelic Policy Quagmire.*

48. **Looking for Graduate Programs.** Thomas B. Roberts, "Psychedelics: Hints on Looking for Graduate Programs" (2007, date estimated), available on Academia website.

49. **production of knowledge should be uninhibited.** Menand, *The Marketplace of Ideas,* 13–14.

CHAPTER 7. WHAT IS PHILOSOPHY'S GREATEST OPPORTUNITY?

1. **insight into depths as yet unspoken.** Alfred North Whitehead, "The Aim of Philosophy," Lecture Nine in *Modes of Thought* (New York: Macmillan, 1938), 237.

2. **Philosophy of psychedelics.** "Philosophy of Psychedelics," Wikipedia.

3. **Alan Watts.** Alan Watts, *The Joyous Cosmology: Adventures in the Chemistry of Consciousness* (New York: Pantheon, 1962).

4. **Aldous Huxley.** Huxley, *The Doors of Perception.*

5. **Breaking Convention.** Breaking Convention website and youtube videos.

6. **online archive.** Roberts and Hruby, *Psychoactive Sacraments.*

7. **William James.** William James, *The Varieties of Religious Experience,* 298.

8. **Hogamus, higamous.** Robert S. de Ropp, *The Master Game: Beyond the Drug Experience* (New York: Delta Books, 1968), 62.

9. **"The Psychedelic Influence on Philosophy."** Sjöstedt-H, "The Hidden Psychedelic History of Philosophy."

10. **Sartre took mescaline.** Riedlinger, "Sartre's Rite of Passage," 105–23.

11. **experience was deeply transformative.** Stokkink, "Psychedelics as a Practice of Truth: A Foucauldian Argument," in Ellens and Roberts, eds., *The Psychedelic Policy Quagmire,* 178.

12. ***Cleansing the Doors of Perception.*** Smith, *Cleansing the Doors of Perception,* 11.

13. **duped historians of philosophy.** Smith, *Cleansing the Doors of Perception,* 11.

14. **psychedelics' influence through the works of thirteen philosophers.** Sjöstedt-H, "The Hidden Psychedelic Influence on Philosophy."

15. **"Empirical Metaphysics."** Smith, *Cleansing the Doors of Perception,* 9–13.

16. **Grof's patients.** Grof, *LSD: Doorway to the Numinous.* Originally pub-

lished in 1975 by Viking Press, New York, under the title *Realms of the Human Unconscious.*

17. **foundational reality.** Ralph W. Hood Jr., ed., "The Facilitation of Religious Experience," in *Handbook of Religious Experience* (Birmingham, Ala.: Religious Education Press, 1995), 570.

18. **produce seemingly realistic experiences.** Winkelman, "An Ontology of Psychedelic Entity Experiences in Evolutionary Psychology and Neurophenomenology," 1–19.

19. **ayahuasca and cognitive psychology.** Shanon, *Antipodes.*

20. **contradictory statements.** Roberts, *The Psychedelic Future of the Mind,* 18.

21. **paradoxicality.** James, *Varieties of Religious Experience,* 298.

22. **reconciliation.** James, *Varieties of Religious Experience,* 298.

23. **top five values.** William R. Miller and Janet C'de Baca, *Quantum Change: When Epiphanies and Sudden Insights Transform Lives* (New York: Guilford Press, 2001), 131.

24. **altruism.** Griffiths et al., "Mystical-type Experiences Occasioned by Psilocybin Mediate the Attribution of Personal Meaning and Spiritual Significance 14 Months Later," 621–32.

25. **values frequently shift away from ego-centered.** Fadiman, *The Psychedelic Explorer's Guide,* 292. See also Roberts, "Raising Values," *The Psychedelic Future of the Mind.*

26. **to modulate one's moral and emotional responses.** Earp, "Psychedelic Moral Enhancement," 415–39.

27. **does healing vary from mindbody state to mindbody state.** Roberts, *Psychedelic Future of the Mind,* 88–101.

28. **seeing what Adam had seen.** Huxley, *The Doors of Perception,* 16.

29. **pure being.** Huxley, *The Doors of Perception,* 33.

30. **Constitutional right.** Roberts, "You Have a Constitutional Right to Psychedelics: Academic Freedom, Personal Conscience, and Psychotechnologies," in Ellens and Roberts, eds., *The Psychedelic Policy Quagmire.*

31. **chilling effect.** Ellens and Roberts, eds., *The Psychedelic Policy Quagmire,* 20–28.

32. **Neurosingularity Project.** Roberts, "Mindapps and the Neurosingularity Project," in Ellens and Roberts, eds., *The Psychedelic Policy Quagmire.*

33. **augmentation of the phenomenal toolkit.** Sjöstedt-H, "The Hidden Psychedelic History of Philosophy."

CHAPTER 8. THE ENTHEOGEN REFORMATION

1. **many of the Psychology, Religion, and Spirituality Series.** Thomas B. Roberts, "Chemical Input, Religious Output—Entheogens: A Pharmatheology Sampler," *Where God and Science Meet, Vol. 3, The Psychology of Religious Experience* (2006); "Multistate and Entheogenic Contributions to the Study of Miracles and Experimental Religious Studies," *Miracles: God, Science, and Psychology of the Paranormal, Vol. 3, Psychological Perspectives* (2008); "Entheogenic Contributions to Self-Transcendence, Healing, Pastoral Counseling, and Evangelism," *The Healing Power of Spirituality: How Faith Helps Humans Survive, Vol. 3, Psychodynamics* (2010); "From the 500-Year Blizzard of Words to Personal Sacred Experiences—The New Religious Era," in Ellens, *Seeking the Sacred with Psychoactive Substances: Chemical Pathways to Spirituality and God, Vol. 1: History and Practices* (2014); "Luther's "A Mighty Fortress Is Our God"—Insights from Grof's Perinatal Theory," *Seeking the Sacred with Psychoactive Substances: Chemical Pathways to Spirituality and God, Vol. 1: History and Practices* (2014).

2. **invention of the printing press.** Karen Armstrong, *The Case for God* (New York: Alfred A. Knopf, 2009), 171.

3. **a strict process of using them.** Johnson, Richards, and Griffiths, "Human Hallucinogen Research," 603–21.

4. **books on the religious uses of psychoactive plants and chemicals.** Roberts and Hruby, *Psychoactive Sacraments.*

5. **"infused contemplation."** Pius XI 1923. On St. Thomas Aquinas. *Strudorum Ducem,* Papal Encyclicals Online.

6. **new religious movement.** "New Religious Movement," Wikipedia.

7. **quest religion.** Association of Religion Data Archives, "Religious Quest," (2018).

8. **'nones,' attending divinity school.** Samuel G. Freedman, "Secular, but Feeling a Call to Divinity School," *New York Times,* Oct. 17, 2015, page A12.

9. **spiritual but not religious.** Michael Lipka and Claire Gecewicz, "More Americans Now Say They're Spiritual but Not Religious," Pew Research Center website, Sept. 6, 2017.

10. **United States Supreme Court issued a unanimous decision.** Earth Erowid, "UDV Wins Supreme Court Decision on Preliminary Injunction," The Vaults of Erowid website, February 21, 2006.

11. **(RFRA) protects the Santo Daime's use of DMT-containing ayahuasca.** Earth Erowid, "Santo Daime Wins Court Decision," The Vaults of Erowid website, February 6, 2012.

12. **infringement of the religious freedom.** "Court of Appeal Amsterdam," (February 28, 2018): page 6, *Bia Labate.*

13. **psychedelic experiences opened the door to Buddhism.** Tart, "Psychedelics on the Path" in Badiner, ed., *Zig Zag Zen Buddhism and Psychedelics,* 167–73.

14. **reader and web survey.** Rick Fields, "A High History of Buddhism," *Tricycle: The Buddhist Review* 6, no. 1 (fall 1996): 42–55.

15. **"Psilocybin-Occasioned Mystical-type Experience in Combination with Meditation . . ."** Griffiths et al., "Psilocybin-Occasioned Mystical-type Experience in Combination with Meditation and Other Spiritual Practices Produces Enduring Positive Changes in Psychological Functioning and in Trait Measures of Prosocial Attitudes and Behaviors," *Journal of Psychopharmacology* 32, no. 1 (2018): 29–69.

16. **"Raising Values."** Roberts, "Raising Values," *The Psychedelic Future of the Mind.*

17. **reformulate rituals, ethics, and organizational activities.** Ellens, ed., *Seeking the Sacred.*

18. ***Drug Policies.*** Kleiman and Caulkins, *Drug Policies.*

19. **the fulfillment of Moses' prayer.** Mark Kleiman, "Mysticism in the Lab," (2011).

20. **God as an ultimate reality.** Griffiths et al., "Mystical-type Experiences Occasioned by Psilocybin Mediate the Attribution of Personal Meaning and Spiritual Significance 14 Months Later," 626.

21. **Eastern and Western, Hindu, Buddhist, Christian, and Sufi.** F. Vaughan, "A Question of Balance: Health and Pathology in New Age Movements" (1987), retrieved from the Council of Spiritual Practices website.

22. **five most spiritually significant experiences.** Griffiths et al., "Mystical-type Experiences Occasioned by Psilocybin Mediate the Attribution of Personal Meaning and Spiritual Significance 14 Months Later," 626.

23. **altruism, sense of well-being, positive attitudes about life.** Griffiths et al., "Mystical-type Experiences Occasioned by Psilocybin Mediate the Attribution of Personal Meaning and Spiritual Significance 14 Months Later," 626.

24. **uncompromising atheists and antireligious crusaders.** Grof, *Realms of the Human Unconscious,* 97–98.

25. **"Experimental Metaphysics."** Smith, *Cleansing the Doors of Perception,* 9–13.

26. **to devise something like the Eleusinian mysteries.** Smith, *Cleansing the Doors of Perception,* 115.

27. **permission for seminary students.** Huston Smith, "Do Drugs Have Religious Import? A Thirty-five-Year Retrospect," in Thomas B. Roberts, ed., *Spiritual Growth with Entheogens: Psychoactive Sacramentals and Human Transformation* (Rochester, Vt.: Park Street Press, 2012), 23.

28. **movements that accent spiritual experience.** Cox, *The Future of Faith,* 10.

29. **an Other moving toward me.** Harvey Cox, *Turning East: The Promise and Peril of the New Orientalism* (New York: Simon and Schuster, 1977), 47–48.

30. **capacity for awe be enhanced by a drug.** Cox, *The Future of Faith,* 24.

31. **deliver us from beliefs.** Huxley, *Island.*

32. **"God in the Flowerpot."** Barnard, *The Mythmakers,* 24.

33. **Personal Meaning and Spiritual Significance.** Griffiths et al., "Psilocybin Can Occasion Mystical-type Experiences Having Substantial and Sustained Personal Meaning and Spiritual Significance."

34. **extensive favorable media coverage.** Council on Spiritual Practices website, "Psilocybin Research" and "2006 Media Coverage," states, "The July 2006 publication of the first Hopkins/CSP psilocybin study drew media attention around the globe (including some 300 print articles according to Goggle, plus magazine, radio, and TV coverage)."

35. **Hopkins Scientists Seek Religious Leaders.** "Religious Leader Study," Council on Spiritual Practices website.

36. **wisdom and vitality that may illumine.** Richards, *Sacred Knowledge,* 27.

37. **extend legal authorization to retreat and research centers.** Richards, *Sacred Knowledge,* 177.

CONCLUSION. MULTISTATE THEORY AS A VITAL PARADIGM FOR THE FUTURE

1. **requirements for a new paradigm.** Kuhn, *Scientific Revolutions.*

2. **especially to the intellectual.** Huxley, *The Doors of Perception,* 73.

APPENDIX A. SYLLABUS FOR
A PSYCHEDELIC CLASS

1. **The Psychedelic Explorer's Guide.** Fadiman, *The Psychedelic Explorer's Guide.*

2. **Heffter website.** Heffter Research Institute website.

3. **CYA.** "Cover Your Ass," Wikipedia.

4. *Realms of the Human Unconscious.* Grof, *Realms of the Human Unconscious.*

5. *Psychedelic Drugs Reconsidered.* Lester Grinspoon and James B. Bakalar, *Psychedelic Drugs Reconsidered* (New York: Basic Books, 1979).

Bibliography

This bibliography includes only selected items. For a complete list of sources referenced, please see the notes.

Barnard, Mary. *The Mythmakers*. Athens: Ohio University Press, 1966.

Campbell, Joseph. *The Hero with a Thousand Faces*. Princeton, N.J.: Princeton University Press, 1973. Originally published in 1949.

———. *Myths to Live By*. New York: Viking, 1972.

Chalmers, David. "Facing Up to the Problem of Consciousness." *Journal of Consciousness Studies* 2, no. 3 (1995): 200–19.

Cox, Harvey. *The Future of Faith*. New York: HarperCollins, 2009.

Earp, Brian. "Psychedelic Moral Enhancement." In Hauskeller, M. and L. Coyne, eds. *Royal Institute of Philosophy Supplement*. Cambridge: Cambridge University Press.

Ellens, J. Harold, ed. *Seeking the Sacred with Psychoactive Substances: Chemical Paths to Spirituality and to God* 2 vols. Santa Barbara, Calif.: ABC-CLIO, 2014.

Ellens, J. Harold, and Thomas B. Roberts, eds., *The Psychedelic Policy Quagmire: Health, Law, Freedom, and Society*. Santa Barbara, Calif.: Preger/ABC-CLIO, 2015.

Fadiman, James. *The Psychedelic Explorer's Guide: Safe, Therapeutic, and Sacred Journeys*. Rochester, Vt.: Park Street Press, 2011.

Griffiths, Roland R., William A. Richards, Matthew Johnson, Una D. McCann, and Robert T. Jesse. "Mystical-type Experiences Occasioned by Psilocybin Mediate the Attribution of Personal Meaning and Spiritual Significance

14 Months Later." *Journal of Psychopharmacology* 22, no. 6 (2008): 621–32.

———. "Psilocybin Can Occasion Mystical-type Experiences Having Substantial and Sustained Personal Meaning and Spiritual Significance." *Psychopharmacology* 187, no. 3 (2006): 268–83.

Grinspoon, Lester and James Bakalar. *Psychedelic Reflections*. New York: Human Sciences Press, 1983.

Grof, Stanislav. *LSD: Doorway to the Numinous*. Rochester, Vt.: Park Street Press, 2009. Originally published in New York: Viking Press, 1975, under the title *Realms of the Human Unconscious*.

———. *LSD Psychotherapy*. Pomona, Calif.: Hunter House, 1980. Also published in Santa Cruz, Calif. by MAPS in 2001.

———. "The Perinatal Roots of Wars, Revolutions, and Totalitarianism." *Journal of Psychohistory* 4, no. 3 (1977): 269–308.

Harman, Willis W., Robert H. McKim, Robert E. Mogar, James Fadiman, and Myron J. Stolaroff. "Psychedelic Agents in Creative Problem Solving: A Pilot Study." *Psychological Reports* 19 (1966): 211–27.

Huxley, Aldous. *The Doors of Perception*. New York: Harper & Row, 1954.

———. *Island*. New York: Harper & Row, 1962.

James, William. *The Varieties of Religious Experience: A Study in Human Nature*. New York: New American Library, 1958. Originally published in 1902.

Johnson, Matthew, William A. Richards, and Roland Griffiths. "Human Hallucinogen Research: Guidelines for Safety." *Journal of Psychopharmacology* 22, no. 6 (2008): 603–21.

Kleiman, Mark and Jonathan Caulkins. *Drug Policies: What Everyone Needs to Know*. Oxford, UK: Oxford University Press, 2011.

Kuhn, Thomas. *The Structure of Scientific Revolutions*. Chicago: University of Chicago Press, 1962.

Luke, David. *Otherworlds: Psychedelics and Exceptional Human Experience*. London: Muswell Hill Press, 2017.

MacLean, Katherine A., Matthew W. Johnson, and Roland R. Griffiths. "Mystical Experiences Occasioned by the Hallucinogen Psilocybin Lead to increases in the Personality Domain of Openness." *Journal of Psychopharmacology* 25, no. 11 (2011): 1453–61.

Maslow, Abraham H. *The Farther Reaches of Human Nature*. New York: Viking Press, 1971.

Menand, Louis. *The Marketplace of Ideas*. New York: W. W. Norton, 2010.

Merlin, M. D. "Archaeological Evidence for the Tradition of Psychoactive Plant Use in the Old World." *Economic Botany* 57, no. 3 (2003): 295–323.

Nichols, Dave. "(1990–2000). From Eleusis to PET Scans: The Mysteries of Psychedelics." *MAPS Bulletin* 9, no. 4, 50–55.

Petri, Giovanni, Paul Expert, F. Turkheimer, Robin Carhart-Harris, David J. Nutt, Peter Hellyer, and Francesco Vaccarino. "Homological Scaffolds of Brain Functional Networks." *Journal of the Royal Society Interface* 11 (2014): 101.

Pollan, Michael. "The Trip Treatment: Research into Psychedelics, Shut Down for Decades, Is Now Yielding Exciting Results." *The New Yorker,* February 9, 2015, 36–47.

Richards, William A. *Sacred Knowledge: Psychedelics and Religious Experience.* New York: Columbia University Press, 2015.

Riedlinger, Thomas J., ed. *The Sacred Mushroom Seeker: Tributes to R. Gordon Wasson.* Rochester, Vt.: Park Street Press, 1997.

Riedlinger, Thomas J. "Sartre's Rite of Passage." *The Journal of Transpersonal Psychology* 14, no. 2 (1982): 105–23.

Roberts, Thomas B. "Brainstorm: A Psychological Odyssey." *Journal of Humanistic Psychology* 26, no. 1 (1986): 126–36.

———. "A Humanistic Social Typology with Applications to a Study of Higher Education and Suggestions for a Social Theory." Unpublished doctoral dissertation, Stanford University, 1972.

———. *Psychedelic Horizons.* Exeter, England: Imprint Academic, 2006.

———. *The Psychedelic Future of the Mind: How Entheogens Are Enhancing Cognition, Boosting Intelligence, and Raising Values* . Rochester, Vt.: Park Street Press, 2013.

Roberts, Thomas B., and P. Hruby. *Psychoactive Sacraments: An Entheogen Chrestomathy.* Council of Spiritual Practices, 1995, 2001.

Rothen, Nicholas, David J. Schwartzman, Daniel Bor, and Anil K. Seth. "Coordinated Neural, Behavioral, and Phenomenological Changes in Perceptual Plasticity through Overtraining of Synesthetic Association." *Neuropsychologia* 11 (2018): 151–62.

Rudgley, Richard. *Essential Substances: A Cultural History of Intoxicants in Society.* New York: Kodansha International, 1994.

Sessa, Ben. *The Psychedelic Renaissance: Reassessing the Role of Psychedelic Drugs in 21st Century Psychiatry and Society,* 2nd ed. London: Muswell Hill Press, 2017.

Shanon, Benny. *The Antipodes of the Mind: Charting the Phenomenology of the Ayahuasca Experience.* Oxford: Oxford University Press, 2002.

Siff, Stephen. *Acid Hype: American News Media and Psychedelic Experience.* Urbana: University of Illinois Press, 2015.

Sjöstedt-H, Peter. "The Hidden Psychedelic History of Philosophy: Plato, Nietzsche, and 11 Other Philosophers Who Used Mind-Altering Drugs." *High Existence* magazine website (2016).

Smith, Huston. *Cleansing the Doors of Perception: The Religious Significance of Entheogenic Plants and Chemicals.* New York: Tarcher/Putnam, 2000.

———. *Forgotten Truth: The Common Vision of the World's Religions.* New York: Harper & Row, 1976.

Solon, Olivia. "Under Pressure, Silicon Valley Workers Turn to LSD Microdosing." *Wired* magazine website, August 24, 2016.

Sternberg, Robert. *The Triarchic Mind: A New Theory of Human Intelligence.* New York: Penguin, 1988.

Tart, Charles T. *States of Consciousness.* New York: E. P. Dutton, 1975.

———. "Psychedelics on the Path: Help or Hindrance?" In Allan Badiner, ed., *Zig Zag Zen Buddhism and Psychedelics,* San Francisco: Chronicle Books, 2002.

Waldman, Ayelet. *A Really Good Day: How Microdosing Made a Mega Difference in My Mood, My Marriage, and My Life.* New York: Knopf, 2017.

Walsh, Roger and Charles C. Grob, eds. *Higher Wisdom: Eminent Elders Explore the Continuing Impact of Psychedelics.* Albany: State University of New York Press, 2005.

Wasson, R. Gordon. "Seeking the Magic Mushroom." *LIFE,* May 20, 1957, 100–20.

Waters, Roger, David Appleby, and Gerald Scarfe. *Pink Floyd: The Wall.* New York: Avon Books, 1982.

Wilson, Edward Osborne. *Consilience: The Unity of Knowledge.* New York: Knopf, 1998.

Winkelman, Michael James. "An Ontology of Psychedelic Entity Experiences in Evolutionary Psychology and Neurophenomenology." *Journal of Psychedelic Studies* (March 2018):1–19.

Index